Jobseeker's Guide
Fourth Edition

Navigating the Federal Job System
For Transitioning Military Personnel and
Family Members of Active Duty Military

By Kathryn Troutman
With Paulina Chen, Designer

The
Resume Place

89 Mellor Avenue
Baltimore, MD 21228
www.resume-place.com

The Resume Place, Inc.
Federal Career Publishers
89 Mellor Avenue, Baltimore, MD 21228
Phone: 888-480-8265
www.resume-place.com
Email: resume@resume-place.com

Printed in the United States of America
Library of Congress Control Number: 2010929446

Jobseeker's Guide, Ten Steps to a Federal Job, 4th Ed.
ISBN: 978-0-9824190-3-8

We have been careful to provide accurate federal job search information in this book, but it is
possible that errors and omissions may have been introduced.

Attention Transition Counselors, Veterans' Representatives, Workforce Counselors, Career
Counselors: The Jobseeker's Guide is a training program "handout" to support the Ten Steps to a
Federal Job Workshops and PowerPoint program, which is taught at military bases, universities,
one-stops, and DoD agencies worldwide. To be licensed to teach the Ten Steps curriculum as a
Certified Federal Job Search Trainer or Certified Federal Career Coach Programs, go to www.
resume-place.com for information on our train the trainer program. Developed in 2002, more than
350 career professionals are licensed to teach Ten Steps with this guide as the handout.

AUTHOR'S NOTES: Sample resumes are real but fictionalized. All federal applicants have given
permission for their resumes to be used as samples for this publication.
Privacy policy is strictly enforced.

PUBLICATION TEAM:
Cover and Interior Page Design: Paulina Chen
Editors: Paulina Chen, Sandra Lee Keppley
Federal Resume Sample Designs: Kathryn Troutman
KSA / Questionnaire Chapter: Diane Hudson-Burns
Indexer: L. Pilar Wyman

about VETERANS

"For their service and sacrifice, warm words of thanks

from a grateful nation are more than warranted, but they aren't nearly enough. We also owe our veterans the care they were promised and the benefits that they have earned. We have a sacred trust with those who wear the uniform of the United States of America. It's a commitment that begins at enlistment, and it must never end. But we know that for too long, we've fallen short of meeting that commitment. Too many wounded warriors go without the care that they need. Too many veterans don't receive the support that they've earned. Too many who once wore our nation's uniform now sleep in our nation's streets."

– President Obama, March 19, 2009
www.whitehouse.gov/issues/veterans

Dear Federal Jobseekers and Career Trainers/Advisors,

The U.S. government is now promoting special hiring and added preference programs for former military personnel, family members, and wounded warriors. It is a promising and exciting time to move into the federal government.

Take for example, my favorite new idea about how to make federal jobs for veterans become a reality:

Agency Directory - Veteran Employment Program Offices
http://veterans.gov/AgencyDirectory/index.aspx

You will find on this website a real contact list for individuals who are working on creating more jobs for veterans. I recommend contacting these individuals by email rather than phone call.

But remember that you will STILL have to write a federal resume to demonstrate your qualifications. This book is designed to help you learn resume styles, targeted writing techniques, and online application systems. I designed the Jobseeker's Guide based on my popular Ten Steps to a Federal Job™ curriculum, with special consideration to military personnel and family members. You will find that each step provides critical information to help you understand and master the hiring process.

This fourth edition contains important federal job information updates, such as changes in online builders, the elimination of traditional KSA essays, and an expanded section in the front of the book about special hiring programs and noncompetitive appointment programs for military and family members.

Good luck with your federal job search,
Kathryn Troutman

In this preface you will find:

- **A quick overview of the Ten Steps to a Federal Job**
  Getting a federal job is not just writing a resume. It is a long process with many steps.

- **Participant Introductions**
  If you are teaching this in a class, use this worksheet to help the particpants get to know each other.

- **Accomplishments Freewriting**
  Start the course off by remember some of your best accomplishments

- **Special Hiring Programs**
  A short summary of the different federal hiring programs applying to veterans and family members.

This is a federal job search campaign – not just a resume and application for a job. The most determined and persevering veterans and spouses WILL get hired into a stable career civilian position in government following all of these ten steps.

1. **Review the federal job process.** Start your federal job search with critical federal job information. Find out which agencies, job titles, and grade levels are best suited for you.

2. **Your network.** Even with government, who you know is important. This information will remind you that your family, friends, and acquaintances may be a lead to a job in government. Learn strategies to introduce yourself and your job goals.

3. **Research vacancy announcements on USAJOBS.** Learn the fastest way to search for federal jobs on USAJOBS. Search for geographic location and salary first, then drill down to the jobs that sound right for you. You can't write a good federal resume without a target vacancy announcement – even if the announcement is a sample to get you started.

4. **Analyze your core competencies.** In addition to technical keywords and qualifications, your basic core competencies can help you stand out. Are you flexible, customer-focused, and creative? Do you demonstrate excellent team membership abilities, and work well under deadlines? Technical, specialized skills + great interpersonal skills = Best Qualified!

5. **Analyze vacancy announcements for keywords.** Learn how to find 10 or more keywords in each announcement for your federal resume. Look for the keywords in Duties, Qualifications, Specialized Experience and KSA lists. Add the keywords into your resume to make it readable, focused, and impressive.

6. **Write your Outline Format and paper federal resumes.** Feature your top skills and accomplishments for each position with keywords. Master the two formats: the Outline Format for online builders, and the paper format for interviews, email attachments, and browser uploads.

7. **KSAs in your federal resume and assessment questionnaires.** The "rated and ranked" KSAs are almost gone, but various "how to apply" instructions may still list KSAs that should be covered in the resume. You will also find Assessment Questionnaires with Yes-No and Multiple Choice questions.

8. **Apply for jobs with automated recruitment systems.** Carefully read the "how to apply" instructions, which could be different for each announcement. Get ready to copy and paste your resume into builders, answer questions, write short essays, and fax or upload your docuemnts.

9. **Track and follow up your applications.** Don't just send in your application and forget about it; you have to manage your federal job search campaign. Learn how to call the personnel office to find out critical information for improving your future applications. Find out how to get your application score.

10. **Interview for a federal job.** Get tips to improve your chances with different types of interviews. Tell your best stories about your accomplishments and leadership skills. Be personable, passionate about the job, and sharp. with our list of techniques.

Take a few minutes to write your information and accomplishments.

Please answer these questions:

What is your current or last job title?

What would you like to learn in this workshop?

Accomplishment Freewriting:

Please describe an accomplishment from your current position or recent volunteer work. Accomplishments are critical for your federal resume, assessment questionnaire essays / examples, and for your behavior-based interviews.

Please write at least three sentences here about your accomplishment:

LOGISTICS MANAGER OF THE YEAR

TOP OFFICER RECRUITING PROGAM OF THE YEAR

FLIGHT LOGISTICS NCO OF THE QTR

4X SENIOR RECRUITER AWARD

The bold type indicates the type of accomplishment this applicant has achieved the skills and competencies they have demonstrated through their outstanding service.

DEMONSTRATES HIGH PERFORMANCE, SAFETY, HIGH PROFICIENCY LEVEL

As a Pilot in Command and Flight Lead (CW2), US Army, Aviation Regiment, I successfully arrived at the landing one within 30 seconds of the planned time and within 10 meters, while factoring in refuel stops, crew rest policies, and uncontrollable variables, such as weather and enemy activities.

DEMONSTRATES TRAINING, SAFETY, TEAM WORK

As a USCG Sector WaterWays Boarding Security Team Member (Gunner's Mate, E-5) in Honolulu, HI, I served as a Fire Arms Instructor for Federal Law Enforcement Teams. I taught handling, operation, and maintenance of small arms weapons, ammunition, and pyrotechnics. I am proficient in the use of 9 mm Beretta, M16 A1 rifle, and riot shotgun as well as ordnance/gunnery equipment mechanical, electrical, and hydraulic maintenance.

DEMONSTRATES PHYSICAL SECURITY EXCELLENCE

As a Criminal Investigative Division Special Agent, US Army Reserve, I was awarded for five years for 100 percent inventory physical security inspections.

DEMONSTRATES OPERATIONS EFFICIENCY AND MISSION SUCCESS

In 2007, as an Operations Officer with the 77th Personnel Services Battalion, Armed Forces Overseas Germany, I developed a management system that increased efficiency of processing $90,000 in business travel vouchers and achieved 100 percent accuracy during the annual 2002 audit.

During this time, I single-handedly coordinated all Force Protection missions for all subordinate companies in five different communities. This involved expert planning and executing of five movements involving a total of 150 personnel to Albania, Macedonia, Kosovo, Turkey, and Iraq. Training and assessing these personnel prior to their movement resulted in all personnel accomplishing their jobs and returning safely home.

DEMONSTRATES MARKETING EXPERTISE

As an administrative assistant and placement recruiter with Adecco Placement, I designed and implemented six-week blitz marketing campaign using pre-printed flyers and brochures, phone calls, and personal notes to reach hiring authorities within target businesses. Tracked marketing campaign results for analysis.

DEMONSTRATES SERVICES TO VETERANS, LOGISTICS AND SAFETY

While on MedHold at Walter Reed Army Medical Hospital, I interned with the VA and assisted Vets in New Orleans with escaping the Katrina Hurricane. I coordinated the relocation of 300+ veterans from the Armed Forces Retirement Home in Gulfport, Mississippi to the U.S. Solders' and Airmen's Home located in Washington, D.C. during the aftermath of Hurricane Katrina. Established phone card and clothing rives to ensure that each veteran had sufficient clothing and was able to communicate with their family and friends to ensure they were aware of the veteran's current living arrangements. Awarded the Humanitarian Service Medal and the Mississippi Emergency Service Medal for my actions.

Are you or your spouse eligible for any special preferences or do you or your spouse belong to any special group of people? How about other members of your household?

For Everyone

Federal Career Intern Program (FCIP)

What it provides: The FCIP is a two-year training program that can lead to permanent employment in the federal government upon successful completion of program requirements. Trainees receive the same pay and benefits as regular federal employees at the same grade level. They are eligible to receive pay increases and be promoted while in the program. One advantage of the program is its flexibility to accelerate promotions. That is, agencies may promote a trainee without regard to time-in-grade requirements (i.e., the requirement to spend a whole year in grade before promotion to the next higher grade).

When it is used: It is used to hire trainees in any occupation in the GS-5, 7, or 9 grade levels.

Who is eligible: The program is open to anyone who qualifies for the grade of the position for which he/she applied.

Why a hiring manager uses FCIP: It is quick and easy to implement. It is the closest to on-the-spot hiring.

Direct Hire

Agencies use direct hire authority when there is a shortage of qualified candidates (i.e., an agency is unable to identify qualified candidates despite extensive recruitment or extended announcement periods), or when an agency has a critical hiring need, such as an emergency or unanticipated event, or changed mission requirements. Its very nature allows agencies to forgo rating and ranking qualified candidates or applying veterans' preference.

Direct hire provides agencies a quick way to hire individuals in the competitive service. Positions filled through direct hire are posted on USAJOBS.

Certain agencies have direct hire authority for certain occupations. However, OPM allows the government-wide use of direct hire authority for the following occupations:

- Information technology management related to security
- X-ray technicians
- Medical officers, nurses, and pharmacists
- Positions involved in Iraqi reconstruction efforts that require fluency in Arabic
- Acquisition positions covered under title 41 (effective through September 30, 2012)

For Veterans

Veterans Recruitment Appointment (VRA) (Formerly Veterans Readjustment Appointment)

What it provides: VRA allows appointment of eligible veterans up to the GS-11 or equivalent. Veterans are hired under excepted appointments to positions that are otherwise in the competitive service. After the individual satisfactorily completes two years of service, the veteran must be converted noncompetitively to a career or career-conditional appointment.

When it is used: VRA is used for filling entry-level to mid-level positions.

Who is eligible: VRA eligibility applies to the following veterans:

- Disabled veterans;
- Veterans who served on active duty in the Armed Forces during a war declared by Congress, or in a campaign or expedition for which a campaign badge has been authorized;
- Veterans who, while serving on active duty in the Armed Forces, participated in a military operation for which the Armed Forces Service Medal was awarded; and
- Veterans separated from active duty within three years.

30 Percent or More Disabled Veterans

What it provides: This authority enables a hiring manager to appoint an eligible candidate to any position for which he or she is qualified, without competition. Unlike the VRA, there's no grade-level limitation. Initial appointments are time-limited, lasting more than 60 days; however, the manager can noncompetitively convert the individual to permanent status at any time during the time-limited appointment.

When it is used: This authority is a good tool for filling positions at any grade level quickly.

Who is eligible: Eligibility applies to the following categories:

- Disabled veterans who were retired from active military service with a disability rating of 30 percent or more; and
- Disabled veterans rated by the Dept. of Veterans Affairs (VA) (within the preceding year) as having a compensable service-connected disability of 30% or more.

Veterans Employment Opportunities Act of 1998 (VEOA)

What it provides: This gives eligible veterans access to jobs otherwise available only to status employees. Veterans are not accorded preference as a factor but are allowed to compete for job opportunities that are not offered to other external candidates. A VEOA eligible who is selected will be given a career or career-conditional appointment.

When it is used: Agencies may appoint VEOA eligibles who have competed under agency merit promotion announcements when they are recruiting from outside their workforce.

Who is eligible: VEOA eligibility applies to the following categories of veterans:

- Preference eligibles; and
- Service personnel separated after 3 or more years of continuous active service performed under honorable conditions.

For Spouses and Other Family Members

For more detail about the programs listed below for spouses and family members, you can download the entire article from Resume Place website at www.resume-place.com/pdfs/ Spouse Preference Article Jan 2010.pdf.

Military Spouse Employment Preference (MSP)

What it provides: MSP provides priority in the employment selection process for military spouses who are relocating as a result of their military spouse's PCS. Spouse preference may be used for most vacant positions in DoD and applies only within the commuting area of the permanent duty station of the sponsor. Spouses may apply for MSP as early as 30 days prior to your reporting date at the new duty station.

When it is used: 1) Placements into competitive civil service vacancies in the 50 states, the Territories, the Possessions, and the District of Columbia; 2) Employment in Foreign areas; 3) Non-appropriated Fund (NAF); 4) Noncompetitive appointments in the civil service for spouses of certain members of the armed forces.

Who is eligible: This preference does not apply to separation or retirement moves. Spouses must be found best qualified for the position and may exercise preference no more than one time per permanent relocation of the sponsor. (If you accept a position with time limitations you do not lose your MSP; i.e., temporary, term, intermittent, or NAF with flexible work schedules).

Noncompetitive Appointment of Certain Military Spouses

What it provides: As of 9/11/09, federal agencies were granted the authority to hire "qualified" military spouses without going through the competitive process. Spouses can find out about job opportunities by going to USAJOBS or websites of specific agencies.

When it is used: The use of this authority is discretionary by federal agencies and the hiring managers. The authority is not limited to specific positions or grade levels but spouses must meet the same requirements as other applicants, to include qualification requirements. Spouses are not provided any "hiring preference" nor does it create an entitlement to federal jobs over other qualified applicants. It is the applicant's responsibility to apply for a job and request consideration for employment under this authority as a military spouse.

Who is eligible:
- Spouses of service members serving on PCS for 180 days or more (provided the spouse relocates to the member's new permanent duty station)
- Spouses of retired service members (who retired under Chapter 61, Title 10, USA), with a disability rating of 100% at the time of retirement
- Spouses of former service members who retired or were released and have a 100% disability rating from the VA
- Un-remarried widows or widowers of armed forces members killed while serving on active duty.

Derived Veteran's Preference

What it provides: By law, veterans who are disabled or who served on active duty in the Armed Forces during certain specified time periods or in military campaigns are entitled to preference over others in competitive external hiring. When a veteran is not able to use their federal employment preference, then the preference can essentially "pass on" to his or her spouse, widow, or mother. The eligible applicant receives an additional ten points to a passing examination score or rating.

When it is used: This preference is based on service of a veteran who is not able to use the federal employment preference. This authority is not related to the MSP described above.

Who is eligible: Spouses, widows, widowers, or mothers of veterans who are unable to work as a result of their service-related disability or have died while on active duty. Both a mother and a spouse (including widow or widower) may be entitled to preference on the basis of the same veteran's service if they both meet the requirements. However, neither may receive preference if the veteran is living and is qualified for Federal employment.

Military Spouses Internship Program

For a limited number of positions through the end of FY2010, federal agencies can hire a military spouse and DoD will pay for one year of salary, benefits, and training.

More information: www.cpms.osd.mil/milspouse/milspouse_index.aspx

Tens of thousands of federal government jobs are posted on USAJOBS alone every day. Which ones will you appy for? In this step, get off to a running start with your job search by getting answers to the three most important questions.

Which job titles do you qualify for?

On pages 21-29, determine if you qualify for a certain job title or series. You can review the list of 32 major occupations and 455 job series in government. We've also included a list of new job titles that are not in the Occupational Standards. New jobs are created everyday with new agencies and missions!

Which agencies are good matches for you?

We recommend that you review the list of agencies to determine your top five agencies of consideration. See the list on pages 16-20. This way you can focus your resume toward a particular federal agency mission and service.

Which grades or salary levels do you qualify for?

Check out pages 30-33 on how to determine your grade or salary level by analyzing your education, training, certifications, years of experience, and specialized knowledge. You will learn how to interpret the pay bands that are posted on many vacancy announcements. The pay bands are bands of grades with large ranges of salary.

Use this worksheet to set your federal job search goals.

TARGET AGENCIES

What are your target agencies?

TARGET JOB TITLES AND SERIES

What is your current military job title?

How many years of specialized experience do you have?

What are your top three generalized skills?

What are your top five specialized skills?

Which federal job titles or series seem correct for you?

Where will your experience fit into the PATCO Chart (page 34)?

- Professional
- Specialist or Analyst
- Administrative or Technical
- Clerical
- Other job category

GRADE AND SALARY

What is your current military rank?

What is your current military salary?

What will be your target federal grade level?

What will your salary be, if you apply to a pay band agency?

Check three agencies of your choice.
View entire list at http://www.usa.gov/Agencies/Federal/All_Agencies/index.shtml.

Alphabetical list of organizations in the federal executive, legislative, and judicial branches

A

Administration for Children and Families
Administration on Aging (AOA)
Administrative Office of the U.S. Courts
Advisory Council on Historic Preservation
Agency for Healthcare Research and Quality
Agency for International Development
Agency for Toxic Substances and Disease Registry
Agricultural Marketing Service
Agricultural Research Service
Air Force, Department of
AMTRAK (National Railroad Passenger Corporation)
Animal and Plant Health Inspection Service
Appalachian Regional Commission
Architect of the Capitol
Armed Forces Retirement Home
Arms Control and International Security, Under Secretary for
Army, Department of
Army Corps of Engineers (USACE)

B

Botanic Garden (USBG)
Broadcasting Board of Governors (BBG), (Voice of America, Radio/TV Marti, and more)
Bureau of Alcohol, Tobacco, Firearms, and Explosives (ATF)
Bureau of Economic Analysis
Bureau of Engraving and Printing
Bureau of Indian Affairs
Bureau of Industry and Security
Bureau of International Labor Affairs
Bureau of Labor Statistics
Bureau of Land Management
Bureau of Public Debt
Bureau of Reclamation
Bureau of Transportation Statistics

C

Census Bureau
Center for Nutrition Policy and Promotion
Centers for Disease Control and Prevention (CDC)
Centers for Medicare & Medicaid Services
Central Intelligence Agency (CIA)
Citizenship and Immigration Services Bureau (USCIS)
Civilian Radioactive Waste Management
Coast Guard (USCG)
Commission on Civil Rights
Community Oriented Policing Services
Community Planning and Development
Comptroller of the Currency, Office of the
Congressional Budget Office
Consumer Product Safety Commission (CPSC)
Cooperative State Research, Education, and Extension Service
Corporation for National and Community Service
Council of Economic Advisers
Council on Environmental Quality
Court of Appeals for the Armed Forces
Court of Appeals for the Federal Circuit
Court of Appeals for Veterans Claims
Court of Federal Claims
Court of International Trade
Customs and Border Protection

D

Defense Advanced Research Projects Agency
Defense Commissary Agency

Defense Contract Audit Agency
Defense Contract Management Agency
Defense Finance and Accounting Service
Defense Information Systems Agency
Defense Intelligence Agency (DIA)
Defense Legal Services Agency
Defense Logistics Agency
Defense Nuclear Facilities Safety Board
Defense Security Cooperation Agency
Defense Security Service
Defense Threat Reduction Agency
Department of Agriculture (USDA)
Department of Commerce (DOC)
Department of Defense (DOD)
Department of Education (ED)
Department of Energy (DOE)
Department of Health and Human Services (HHS)
Department of Homeland Security (DHS)
Department of Housing and Urban Development (HUD)
Department of the Interior (DOI)
Department of Justice (DOJ)
Department of Labor (DOL)
Department of State (DOS)
Department of Transportation (DOT)
Department of the Treasury
Department of Veterans Affairs (VA)
Disability Employment Policy, Office of
Drug Enforcement Administration (DEA)

E

Economic and Statistics Administration
Economic, Business and Agricultural Affairs
Economic Development Administration
Economic Research Service
Elementary and Secondary Education, Office of
Employee Benefits Security Administration

Employment and Training Administration
Employment Standards Administration
Energy Efficiency and Renewable Energy
Energy Information Administration
Environmental Management
Environmental Protection Agency (EPA)
Equal Employment Opportunity Commission (EEOC)
Executive Office for Immigration Review

F

Fair Housing and Equal Opportunity, Office of
Faith-Based and Community Initiatives Office
Farm Service Agency (FSA)
Federal Aviation Administration
Federal Bureau of Investigation (FBI)
Federal Bureau of Prisons
Federal Communications Commission (FCC)
Federal Deposit Insurance Corporation (FDIC)
Federal Election Commission (FEC)
Federal Emergency Management Agency (FEMA)
Federal Financing Bank
Federal Highway Administration
Federal Housing Enterprise Oversight
Federal Housing Finance Board
Federal Judicial Center
Federal Labor Relations Authority
Federal Law Enforcement Training Center
Federal Mediation and Conciliation Service
Federal Motor Carrier Safety Administration
Federal Railroad Administration
Federal Reserve System
Federal Trade Commission (FTC)
Federal Transit Administration
Financial Management Service
Fish and Wildlife Service
Food and Drug Administration (FDA)
Food and Nutrition Service
Food Safety and Inspection Service

Check three agencies of your choice.

Foreign Agricultural Service
Forest Service
Fossil Energy

G
Government Accountability Office (GAO)
General Services Administration
Geological Survey (USGS)
Global Affairs
Government National Mortgage Association
Government Printing Office
Grain Inspection, Packers, and Stockyards
    Administration

H
Health Resources and Services Administration
Holocaust Memorial Museum
House of Representatives
House Office of Inspector General
House Office of the Clerk
House Organizations, Commissions, and Task
    Forces

I
Indian Health Service
Industrial College of the Armed Forces
Information Resource Management College
Institute of Museum and Library Services
Internal Revenue Service (IRS)
International Broadcasting Bureau (IBB)
International Trade Administration (ITA)

J
Joint Chiefs of Staff
Joint Forces Staff College
Judicial Circuit Courts of Appeal by Geographic
    Location and Circuit

L
Lead Hazard Control
Legal Services Corporation
Library of Congress

M
Marine Corps
Maritime Administration
Marketing and Regulatory Programs
Marshals Service
Merit Systems Protection Board
Mine Safety and Health Administration
Mineral Management Service
Minority Business Development Agency
Mint
Missile Defense Agency
Multifamily Housing Office

N
National Aeronautics and Space Administration
    (NASA)
National Agricultural Statistics Service
National Archives and Records Administration
    (NARA)
National Capital Planning Commission
National Cemetery Administration
National Communications System
National Council on Disability
National Credit Union Administration
National Defense University
National Drug Intelligence Center
National Endowment for the Arts
National Endowment for the Humanities
National Guard Bureau
National Highway Traffic Safety Administration
National Institute of Standards and Technology
    (NIST)
National Institutes of Health (NIH)
National Labor Relations Board

National Laboratories
National Marine Fisheries
National Mediation Board
National Nuclear Security Administration
National Oceanic and Atmospheric
    Administration (NOAA)
National Park Service
National Science Foundation
National Security Agency/Central Security
    Service
National Technical Information Service
National Telecommunications and Information
    Administration
National Transportation Safety Board (NTSB)
National War College
National Weather Service
Natural Resources Conservation Service
Navy, Department of the
Nuclear Energy, Science and Technology
Nuclear Regulatory Commission
Nuclear Waste Technical Review Board

O

Occupational Safety & Health Administration
    (OSHA)
Office of Government Ethics
Office of Management and Budget (OMB)
Office of National Drug Control Policy (ONDCP)
Office of Personnel Management
Office of Science and Technology Policy
Office of Special Counsel
Office of Thrift Supervision
Overseas Private Investment Corporation

P

Pardon Attorney Office
Parole Commission
Patent and Trademark Office

Peace Corps
Pension Benefit Guaranty Corporation
Policy Development and Research
Political Affairs
Postal Rate Commission
Postal Service (USPS)
Postsecondary Education, Office of
Power Marketing Administrations
Presidio Trust
Public Diplomacy and Public Affairs
Public and Indian Housing

R

Radio and TV Marti (Español)
Radio Free Asia (RFA)
Radio Free Europe/Radio Liberty (RFE/RL)
Railroad Retirement Board
Regulatory Information Service Center
Research and Special Programs Administration
Research, Education, and Economics
Risk Management Agency
Rural Business-Cooperative Service
Rural Development
Rural Housing Service
Rural Utilities Service

S

Science Office
Secret Service
Securities and Exchange Commission (SEC)
Selective Service System
Senate
Small Business Administration (SBA)
Smithsonian Institution
Social Security Administration (SSA)
Social Security Advisory Board
Special Education and Rehabilitative Services
Stennis Center for Public Service

Check three agencies of your choice.

Student Financial Assistance Programs
Substance Abuse and Mental Health Services
    Administration
Supreme Court of the United States
Surface Mining, Reclamation, and Enforcement
Surface Transportation Board

T

Tax Court
Technology Administration
Tennessee Valley Authority
Trade and Development Agency
Transportation Security Administration
Trustee Program

U

U.S. International Trade Commission
U.S. Mission to the United Nations
U.S. National Central Bureau – Interpol
U.S. Trade Representative
Unified Combatant Commands
Uniformed Services University of the Health
    Sciences

V

Veterans Benefits Administration
Veterans Employment and Training Service
Veterans Health Administration
Voice of America (VOA)

W

White House
White House Office of Administration
Women's Bureau

FINDING YOUR JOB TITLES

The government classifies jobs that share common characteristics into general work "groups" and specific "series." The occupations are generally divided into white-collar (General Schedule, or GS) and trades (Wage Grade, or WG) job groups. Use this section to identify possible job fits for your skills and interests.

If you are interested in more detailed information about the work performed by a particular job series, you can research the Position Classification Standards maintained by OPM. The standards and other classification documents are available on OPM's web site, at www.opm.gov/fedclass.

Keep in mind that the classification system explains how a job is assigned a title, occupational series, and grade, and explains the type and level of work done at each grade within an occupation. However, the classification standards do not address how an individual qualifies for a particular job or line of work. Information about qualifications is found in OPM's Qualifications Standards, at www.opm. gov/qualifications.

Carefully reading the qualifications requirements for various occupational series at the different grades will help you make realistic decisions about what jobs to pursue, (title, series, and grade) and may save you from wasting time applying for jobs where you simply don't meet those requirements.

Find your target job titles from this listing of the HANDBOOK OF OCCUPATIONAL GROUPS AND FAMILIES, U.S. Office of Personnel Management Office of Classification, Washington, DC.

GS-000 – MISCELLANEOUS OCCUPATIONS GROUP (NOT ELSEWHERE CLASSIFIED)

This group includes all classes of positions the duties of which are to administer, supervise, or perform work, which cannot be included in other occupational groups either because the duties are unique, or because they are complex and come in part under various groups.

Series in this group are:
GS-006 - Correctional Institution Administration Series
GS-007 - Correctional Officer Series
GS-011 - Bond Sales Promotion Series
GS-018 - Safety and Occupational Health Management Series
GS-019 - Safety Technician Series
GS-020 - Community Planning Series
GS-021 - Community Planning Technician Series
GS-023 - Outdoor Recreation Planning Series
GS-025 - Park Ranger Series
GS-028 - Environmental Protection Specialist Series
GS-029 - Environmental Protection Assistant Series
GS-030 - Sports Specialist Series
GS-050 - Funeral Directing Series
GS-060 - Chaplain Series
GS-062 - Clothing Design Series
GS-072 - Fingerprint Identification Series
GS-080 - Security Administration Series
GS-081 - Fire Protection and Prevention Series
GS-082 - United States Marshal Series
GS-083 - Police Series
GS-084 - Nuclear Materials Courier Series
GS-085 - Security Guard Series
GS-086 - Security Clerical and Assistance Series
GS-090 - Guide Series
GS-095 - Foreign Law Specialist Series
GS-099 - General Student Trainee Series

GS-100 – SOCIAL SCIENCE, PSYCHOLOGY, AND WELFARE GROUP

This group includes all classes of positions the duties of which are to advise on, administer, supervise, or perform research or other professional and scientific work, subordinate technical work, or related clerical work in one or more of the social sciences; in psychology; in social work; in recreational activities; or in the administration of public welfare and insurance programs.

Series in this group are:
GS-101 - Social Science Series
GS-102 - Social Science Aid and Technician Series
GS-105 - Social Insurance Administration Series
GS-106 - Unemployment Insurance Series
GS-107 - Health Insurance Administration Series
GS-110 - Economist Series
GS-119 - Economics Assistant Series
GS-130 - Foreign Affairs Series
GS-131 - International Relations Series
GS-132 - Intelligence Series
GS-134 - Intelligence Aid and Clerk Series
GS-135 - Foreign Agricultural Affairs Series
GS-136 - International Cooperation Series
GS-140 - Manpower Research and Analysis Series
GS-142 - Manpower Development Series
GS-150 - Geography Series
GS-160 - Civil Rights Analysis Series
GS-170 - History Series
GS-180 - Psychology Series
GS-181 - Psychology Aid and Technician Series
GS-184 - Sociology Series
GS-185 - Social Work Series
GS-186 - Social Services Aid and Assistant Series
GS-187 - Social Services Series
GS-188 - Recreation Specialist Series
GS-189 - Recreation Aid and Assistant Series
GS-190 - General Anthropology Series
GS-193 - Archeology Series
GS-199 - Social Science Student Trainee Series

GS-200 – HUMAN RESOURCES MANAGEMENT GROUP

This group includes all classes of positions the duties of which are to advise on, administer, supervise, or perform work involved in the various phases of human resources management.

Series in this group are:
GS-201 - Human Resources Management Series
GS-203 - Human Resources Assistance Series

GS-241 - Mediation Series
GS-243 - Apprenticeship and Training Series
GS-244 - Labor Management Relations Examining
    Series
GS-260 - Equal Employment Opportunity Series
GS-299 - Human Resources Management Student
    Trainee Series

GS-300 – GENERAL ADMINISTRATIVE, CLERICAL, AND OFFICE SERVICES GROUP

This group includes all classes of positions the duties of which are to administer, supervise, or perform work involved in management analysis; stenography, typing, correspondence, and secretarial work; mail and file work; the operation of office appliances; the operation of communications equipment, use of codes and ciphers, and procurement of the most effective and efficient communications services; the operation of microform equipment, peripheral equipment, mail processing equipment, duplicating equipment, and copier/duplicating equipment; and other work of a general clerical and administrative nature.

Series in this group are:
GS-301 - Miscellaneous Administration and Program
    Series
GS-302 - Messenger Series
GS-303 - Miscellaneous Clerk and Assistant Series
GS-304 - Information Receptionist Series
GS-305 - Mail and File Series
GS-309 - Correspondence Clerk Series
GS-312 - Clerk-Stenographer and Reporter Series
GS-313 - Work Unit Supervising Series
GS-318 - Secretary Series
GS-319 - Closed Microphone Reporting Series
GS-322 - Clerk-Typist Series
GS-326 - Office Automation Clerical and Assistance
    Series
GS-332 - Computer Operation Series
GS-335 - Computer Clerk and Assistant Series
GS-340 - Program Management Series
GS-341 - Administrative Officer Series
GS-342 - Support Services Administration Series
GS-343 - Management and Program Analysis Series
GS-344 - Management and Program Clerical and
    Assistance Series

GS-346 - Logistics Management Series
GS-350 - Equipment Operator Series
GS-356 - Data Transcriber Series
GS-357 - Coding Series
GS-360 - Equal Opportunity Compliance Series
GS-361 - Equal Opportunity Assistance Series
GS-382 - Telephone Operating Series
GS-390 - Telecommunications Processing Series
GS-391 - Telecommunications Series
GS-392 - General Telecommunications Series
GS-394 - Communications Clerical Series
GS-399 - Administration and Office Support Student
    Trainee Series

GS-400 – NATURAL RESOURCES MANAGEMENT AND BIOLOGICAL SCIENCES GROUP

This group includes all classes of positions the duties of which are to advise on, administer, supervise, or perform research or other professional and scientific work or subordinate technical work in any of the fields of science concerned with living organisms, their distribution, characteristics, life processes, and adaptations and relations to the environment; the soil, its properties and distribution, and the living organisms growing in or on the soil, and the management, conservation, or utilization thereof for particular purposes or uses.

Series in this group are:
GS-401 - General Natural Resources Management
    and Biological Sciences Series
GS-403 - Microbiology Series
GS-404 - Biological Science Technician Series
GS-405 - Pharmacology Series
GS-408 - Ecology Series
GS-410 - Zoology Series
GS-413 - Physiology Series
GS-414 - Entomology Series
GS-415 - Toxicology Series
GS-421 - Plant Protection Technician Series
GS-430 - Botany Series
GS-434 - Plant Pathology Series
GS-435 - Plant Physiology Series
GS-437 - Horticulture Series
GS-440 - Genetics Series
GS-454 - Rangeland Management Series

Find your target job titles.

GS-455 - Range Technician Series
GS-457 - Soil Conservation Series
GS-458 - Soil Conservation Technician Series
GS-459 - Irrigation System Operation Series
GS-460 - Forestry Series
GS-462 - Forestry Technician Series
GS-470 - Soil Science Series
GS-471 - Agronomy Series
GS-480 - Fish and Wildlife Administration Series
GS-482 - Fish Biology Series
GS-485 - Wildlife Refuge Management Series
GS-486 - Wildlife Biology Series
GS-487 - Animal Science Series
GS-499 - Biological Science Student Trainee Series

GS-500 – ACCOUNTING AND BUDGET GROUP

This group includes all classes of positions the duties of which are to advise on, administer, supervise, or perform professional, technical, or related clerical work of an accounting, budget administration, related financial management or similar nature.

Series in this group are:
GS-501 - Financial Administration and Program Series
GS-503 - Financial Clerical and Technician Series
GS-505 - Financial Management Series
GS-510 - Accounting Series
GS-511 - Auditing Series
GS-512 - Internal Revenue Agent Series
GS-525 - Accounting Technician Series
GS-526 - Tax Specialist Series
GS-530 - Cash Processing Series
GS-540 - Voucher Examining Series
GS-544 - Civilian Pay Series
GS-545 - Military Pay Series
GS-560 - Budget Analysis Series
GS-561 - Budget Clerical and Assistance Series
GS-592 - Tax Examining Series
GS-593 - Insurance Accounts Series
GS-599 - Financial Management Student Trainee Series

GS-600 – MEDICAL, HOSPITAL, DENTAL, AND PUBLIC HEALTH GROUP

This group includes all classes of positions the duties of which are to advise on, administer, supervise or perform research or other professional and scientific work, subordinate technical work, or related clerical work in the several branches of medicine, surgery, and dentistry or in related patient care services such as dietetics, nursing, occupational therapy, physical therapy, pharmacy, and others.

Series in this group are:
GS-601 - General Health Science Series
GS-602 - Medical Officer Series
GS-603 - Physician's Assistant Series
GS-610 - Nurse Series
GS-620 - Practical Nurse Series
GS-621 - Nursing Assistant Series
GS-622 - Medical Supply Aide and Technician Series
GS-625 - Autopsy Assistant Series
GS-630 - Dietitian and Nutritionist Series
GS-631 - Occupational Therapist Series
GS-633 - Physical Therapist Series
GS-635 - Kinesiotherapy Series
GS-636 - Rehabilitation Therapy Assistant Series
GS-637 - Manual Arts Therapist Series
GS-638 - Recreation/Creative Arts Therapist Series
GS-639 - Educational Therapist Series
GS-640 - Health Aid and Technician Series
GS-642 - Nuclear Medicine Technician Series
GS-644 - Medical Technologist Series
GS-645 - Medical Technician Series
GS-646 - Pathology Technician Series
GS-647 - Diagnostic Radiologic Technologist Series
GS-648 - Therapeutic Radiologic Technologist Series
GS-649 - Medical Instrument Technician Series
GS-650 - Medical Technical Assistant Series
GS-651 - Respiratory Therapist Series
GS-660 - Pharmacist Series
GS-661 - Pharmacy Technician Series
GS-662 - Optometrist Series
GS-664 - Restoration Technician Series
GS-665 - Speech Pathology and Audiology Series
GS-667 - Orthotist and Prosthetist Series
GS-668 - Podiatrist Series
GS-669 - Medical Records Administration Series
GS-670 - Health System Administration Series
GS-671 - Health System Specialist Series
GS-672 - Prosthetic Representative Series
GS-673 - Hospital Housekeeping Management Series
GS-675 - Medical Records Technician Series
GS-679 - Medical Support Assistance Series

GS-680 - Dental Officer Series
GS-681 - Dental Assistant Series
GS-682 - Dental Hygiene Series
GS-683 - Dental Laboratory Aid and Technician Series
GS-685 - Public Health Program Specialist Series
GS-688 - Sanitarian Series
GS-690 - Industrial Hygiene Series
GS-696 - Consumer Safety Series
GS-698 - Environmental Health Technician Series
GS-699 - Medical and Health Student Trainee Series

GS-700 - VETERINARY MEDICAL SCIENCE GROUP

This group includes positions that advise on, administer, supervise, or perform professional or technical support work in the various branches of veterinary medical science.

Series in this group are:
GS-701 - Veterinary Medical Science Series
GS-704 - Animal Health Technician Series
GS-799 - Veterinary Student Trainee Series

GS-800 – ENGINEERING AND ARCHITECTURE GROUP

This group includes all classes of positions the duties of which are to advise on, administer, supervise, or perform professional, scientific, or technical work concerned with engineering or architectural projects, facilities, structures, systems, processes, equipment, devices, materials or methods. Positions in this group require knowledge of the science or art, or both, by which materials, natural resources, and power are made useful.

Series in this group are:
GS-801 - General Engineering Series
GS-802 - Engineering Technician Series
GS-803 - Safety Engineering Series
GS-804 - Fire Protection Engineering Series
GS-806 - Materials Engineering Series
GS-807 - Landscape Architecture Series
GS-808 - Architecture Series
GS-809 - Construction Control Technical Series
GS-810 - Civil Engineering Series
GS-817 - Survey Technical Series
GS-819 - Environmental Engineering Series

GS-828 - Construction Analyst Series
GS-830 - Mechanical Engineering Series
GS-840 - Nuclear Engineering Series
GS-850 - Electrical Engineering Series
GS-854 - Computer Engineering Series
GS-855 - Electronics Engineering Series
GS-856 - Electronics Technical Series
GS-858 - Biomedical Engineering Series
GS-861 - Aerospace Engineering Series
GS-871 - Naval Architecture Series
GS-873 - Marine Survey Technical Series
GS-880 - Mining Engineering Series
GS-881 - Petroleum Engineering Series
GS-890 - Agricultural Engineering Series
GS-892 - Ceramic Engineering Series
GS-893 - Chemical Engineering Series
GS-894 - Welding Engineering Series
GS-895 - Industrial Engineering Technical Series
GS-896 - Industrial Engineering Series
GS-899 - Engineering and Architecture Student Trainee Series

GS-900 – LEGAL AND KINDRED GROUP

This group includes all positions that advise on, administer, supervise, or perform work of a legal or kindred nature.

Series in this group are:
GS-901 - General Legal and Kindred Administration Series
GS-904 - Law Clerk Series
GS-905 - General Attorney Series
GS-920 - Estate Tax Examining Series
GS-930 - Hearings and Appeals Series
GS-945 - Clerk of Court Series
GS-950 - Paralegal Specialist Series
GS-958 - Employee Benefits Law Series
GS-962 - Contact Representative Series
GS-963 - Legal Instruments Examining Series
GS-965 - Land Law Examining Series
GS-967 - Passport and Visa Examining Series
GS-986 - Legal Assistance Series
GS-987 - Tax Law Specialist Series
GS-991 - Workers' Compensation Claims Examining Series
GS-993 - Railroad Retirement Claims Examining Series

Find your target job titles.

GS-996 - Veterans Claims Examining Series
GS-998 - Claims Assistance and Examining Series
GS-999 - Legal Occupations Student Trainee Series

GS-1000 – INFORMATION AND ARTS GROUP

This group includes positions which involve professional, artistic, technical, or clerical work in (1) the communication of information and ideas through verbal, visual, or pictorial means, (2) the collection, custody, presentation, display, and interpretation of art works, cultural objects, and other artifacts, or (3) a branch of fine or applied arts such as industrial design, interior design, or musical composition. Positions in this group require writing, editing, and language ability; artistic skill and ability; knowledge of foreign languages; the ability to evaluate and interpret informational and cultural materials; or the practical application of technical or esthetic principles combined with manual skill and dexterity; or related clerical skills.

Series in this group are:
GS-1001 - General Arts and Information Series
GS-1008 - Interior Design Series
GS-1010 - Exhibits Specialist Series
GS-1015 - Museum Curator Series
GS-1016 - Museum Specialist and Technician Series
GS-1020 - Illustrating Series
GS-1021 - Office Drafting Series
GS-1035 - Public Affairs Series
GS-1040 - Language Specialist Series
GS-1046 - Language Clerical Series
GS-1051 - Music Specialist Series
GS-1054 - Theater Specialist Series
GS-1056 - Art Specialist Series
GS-1060 - Photography Series
GS-1071 - Audiovisual Production Series
GS-1082 - Writing and Editing Series
GS-1083 - Technical Writing and Editing Series
GS-1084 - Visual Information Series
GS-1087 - Editorial Assistance Series
GS-1099 - Information and Arts Student Trainee Series

GS-1100 – BUSINESS AND INDUSTRY GROUP

This group includes all classes of positions the duties of which are to advise on, administer, supervise, or perform work pertaining to and requiring a knowledge of business and trade practices, characteristics and use of equipment, products, or property, or industrial production methods and processes, including the conduct of investigations and studies; the collection, analysis, and dissemination of information; the establishment and maintenance of contacts with industry and commerce; the provision of advisory services; the examination and appraisement of merchandise or property; and the administration of regulatory provisions and controls.

Series in this group are:
GS-1101 - General Business and Industry Series
GS-1102 - Contracting Series
GS-1103 - Industrial Property Management Series
GS-1104 - Property Disposal Series
GS-1105 - Purchasing Series
GS-1106 - Procurement Clerical and Technician Series
GS-1107 - Property Disposal Clerical and Technician Series
GS-1130 - Public Utilities Specialist Series
GS-1140 - Trade Specialist Series
GS-1144 - Commissary Management Series
GS-1145 - Agricultural Program Specialist Series
GS-1146 - Agricultural Marketing Series
GS-1147 - Agricultural Market Reporting Series
GS-1150 - Industrial Specialist Series
GS-1152 - Production Control Series
GS-1160 - Financial Analysis Series
GS-1163 - Insurance Examining Series
GS-1165 - Loan Specialist Series
GS-1169 - Internal Revenue Officer Series
GS-1170 - Realty Series
GS-1171 - Appraising Series
GS-1173 - Housing Management Series
GS-1176 - Building Management Series
GS-1199 - Business and Industry Student Trainee Series

GS-1200 – COPYRIGHT, PATENT, AND TRADEMARK GROUP

This group includes all classes of positions the duties of which are to advise on, administer, supervise, or perform professional scientific, technical, and legal work involved in the cataloging and registration of copyrights, in the classification and issuance of patents, in the registration of trademarks, in the prosecution of applications for patents before the Patent Office, and in the giving of advice to Government officials on patent matters.

Series in this group are:
GS-1202 - Patent Technician Series
GS-1210 - Copyright Series
GS-1220 - Patent Administration Series
GS-1221 - Patent Adviser Series
GS-1222 - Patent Attorney Series
GS-1223 - Patent Classifying Series
GS-1224 - Patent Examining Series
GS-1226 - Design Patent Examining Series
GS-1299 - Copyright and Patent Student Trainee Series

GS-1300 – PHYSICAL SCIENCES GROUP

This group includes all classes of positions the duties of which are to advise on, administer, supervise, or perform research or other professional and scientific work or subordinate technical work in any of the fields of science concerned with matter, energy, physical space, time, nature of physical measurement, and fundamental structural particles; and the nature of the physical environment.

Series in this group are:
GS-1301 - General Physical Science Series
GS-1306 - Health Physics Series
GS-1310 - Physics Series
GS-1311 - Physical Science Technician Series
GS-1313 - Geophysics Series
GS-1315 - Hydrology Series
GS-1316 - Hydrologic Technician Series
GS-1320 - Chemistry Series
GS-1321 - Metallurgy Series
GS-1330 - Astronomy and Space Science Series
GS-1340 - Meteorology Series
GS-1341 - Meteorological Technician Series

GS-1350 - Geology Series
GS-1360 - Oceanography Series
GS-1361 - Navigational Information Series
GS-1370 - Cartography Series
GS-1371 - Cartographic Technician Series
GS-1372 - Geodesy Series
GS-1373 - Land Surveying Series
GS-1374 - Geodetic Technician Series
GS-1380 - Forest Products Technology Series
GS-1382 - Food Technology Series
GS-1384 - Textile Technology Series
GS-1386 - Photographic Technology Series
GS-1397 - Document Analysis Series
GS-1399 - Physical Science Student Trainee Series

GS-1400 – LIBRARY AND ARCHIVES GROUP

This group includes all classes of positions the duties of which are to advise on, administer, supervise, or perform professional and scientific work or subordinate technical work in the various phases of library and archival science.

Series in this group are:
GS-1410 - Librarian Series
GS-1411 - Library Technician Series
GS-1412 - Technical Information Services Series
GS-1420 - Archivist Series
GS-1421 - Archives Technician Series
GS-1499 - Library and Archives Student Trainee Series

GS-1500 – MATHEMATICS AND STATISTICS GROUP

This group includes all classes of positions the duties of which are to advise on, administer, supervise, or perform professional and scientific work or related clerical work in basic mathematical principles, methods, procedures, or relationships, including the development and application of mathematical methods for the investigation and solution of problems; the development and application of statistical theory in the selection, collection, classification, adjustment, analysis, and interpretation of data; the development and application of mathematical, statistical, and financial

Find your target job titles.

principles to programs or problems involving life and property risks; and any other professional and scientific or related clerical work requiring primarily and mainly the understanding and use of mathematical theories, methods, and operations.

Series in this group are:
GS-1501 - General Mathematics and Statistics Series
GS-1510 - Actuarial Science Series
GS-1515 - Operations Research Series
GS-1520 - Mathematics Series
GS-1521 - Mathematics Technician Series
GS-1529 - Mathematical Statistics Series
GS-1530 - Statistics Series
GS-1531 - Statistical Assistant Series
GS-1540 - Cryptography Series
GS-1541 - Cryptanalysis Series
GS-1550 - Computer Science Series
GS-1599 - Mathematics and Statistics Student Trainee Series

GS-1600 – EQUIPMENT, FACILITIES, AND SERVICES GROUP

This group includes positions the duties of which are to advise on, manage, or provide instructions and information concerning the operation, maintenance, and use of equipment, shops, buildings, laundries, printing plants, power plants, cemeteries, or other government facilities, or other work involving services provided predominantly by persons in trades, group require technical or managerial knowledge and ability, plus a practical knowledge of trades, crafts, or manual labor operations.

Series in this group are:
GS-1601 - Equipment, Facilities, and Services Series
GS-1603 - Equipment, Facilities, and Services Assistance Series
GS-1630 - Cemetery Administration Services Series
GS-1640 - Facility Operations Services Series
GS-1654 - Printing Services Series
GS-1658 - Laundry Operations Services Series
GS-1667 - Food Services Series
GS-1670 - Equipment Services Series
GS-1699 – Equipment, Facilities, and Services Student Trainee Series

GS-1700 – EDUCATION GROUP

This group includes positions that involve administering, managing, supervising, performing, or supporting education or training work when the paramount requirement of the position is knowledge of, or skill in, education, training, or instruction processes.

Series in this group are:
GS-1701 - General Education and Training Series
GS-1702 - Education and Training Technician Series
GS-1710 - Education and Vocational Training Series
GS-1712 - Training Instruction Series
GS-1715 - Vocational Rehabilitation Series
GS-1720 - Education Program Series
GS-1725 - Public Health Educator Series
GS-1730 - Education Research Series
GS-1740 - Education Services Series
GS-1750 - Instructional Systems Series
GS-1799 - Education Student Trainee Series

GS-1800 – INVESTIGATION GROUP

This group includes all classes of positions the duties of which are to advise on, administer, supervise, or perform investigation, inspection, or enforcement work primarily concerned with alleged or suspected offenses against the laws of the United States, or such work primarily concerned with determining compliance with laws and regulations.

Series in this group are:
GS-1801 - General Inspection, Investigation, and Compliance Series
GS-1802 - Compliance Inspection and Support Series
GS-1810 - General Investigating Series
GS-1811 - Criminal Investigating Series
GS-1812 - Game Law Enforcement Series
GS-1815 - Air Safety Investigating Series
GS-1816 - Immigration Inspection Series
GS-1822 - Mine Safety and Health Series
GS-1825 - Aviation Safety Series
GS-1831 - Securities Compliance Examining Series
GS-1850 - Agricultural Commodity Warehouse Examining Series
GS-1854 - Alcohol, Tobacco and Firearms Inspection Series
GS-1862 - Consumer Safety Inspection Series

GS-1863 - Food Inspection Series
GS-1864 - Public Health Quarantine Inspection Series
GS-1881 - Customs and Border Protection Interdiction Series
GS-1884 - Customs Patrol Officer Series
GS-1889 - Import Specialist Series
GS-1890 - Customs Inspection Series
GS-1894 - Customs Entry and Liquidating Series
GS-1895 - Customs and Border Protection Series
GS-1896 - Border Patrol Agent Series
GS-1897 - Customs Aid Series
GS-1899 - Investigation Student Trainee Series

GS-1900 – QUALITY ASSURANCE, INSPECTION, AND GRADING GROUP

This group includes all classes of positions the duties of which are advise on, supervise, or perform administrative or technical work primarily concerned with the quality assurance or inspection of material, facilities, and processes; or with the grading of commodities under official standards.
Series in this group are:
GS-1910 - Quality Assurance Series
GS-1980 - Agricultural Commodity Grading Series
GS-1981 - Agricultural Commodity Aid Series
GS-1999 - Quality Inspection Student Trainee Series

GS-2000 – SUPPLY GROUP

This group includes positions that involve work concerned with furnishing all types of supplies, equipment, material, property (except real estate), and certain services to components of the federal government, industrial, or other concerns under contract to the government, or receiving supplies from the federal government. Included are positions concerned with one or more aspects of supply activities from initial planning, including requirements analysis and determination, through acquisition, cataloging, storage, distribution, utilization to ultimate issues for consumption or disposal. The work requires a knowledge of one or more elements or parts of a supply system, and/or supply methods, policies, or procedures.

Series in this group are:
GS-2001 - General Supply Series
GS-2003 - Supply Program Management Series
GS-2005 - Supply Clerical and Technician Series
GS-2010 - Inventory Management Series
GS-2030 - Distribution Facilities and Storage Management Series

GS-2032 - Packaging Series
GS-2050 - Supply Cataloging Series
GS-2091 - Sales Store Clerical Series
GS-2099 - Supply Student Trainee Series

GS-2100 – TRANSPORTATION GROUP

This group includes all classes of positions the duties of which are to advise on, administer, supervise, or perform clerical, administrative, or technical work involved in the provision of transportation service to the government, the regulation of transportation utilities by the government, or the management of government-funded transportation programs, including transportation research and development projects.

Series in this group are:
GS-2101 - Transportation Specialist Series
GS-2102 - Transportation Clerk and Assistant Series
GS-2110 - Transportation Industry Analysis Series
GS-2121 - Railroad Safety Series
GS-2123 - Motor Carrier Safety Series
GS-2125 - Highway Safety Series
GS-2130 - Traffic Management Series
GS-2131 - Freight Rate Series
GS-2135 - Transportation Loss and Damage Claims Examining Series
GS-2144 - Cargo Scheduling Series
GS-2150 - Transportation Operations Series
GS-2151 - Dispatching Series
GS-2152 - Air Traffic Control Series
GS-2154 - Air Traffic Assistance Series
GS-2161 - Marine Cargo Series
GS-2181 - Aircraft Operation Series
GS-2183 - Air Navigation Series
GS-2185 - Aircrew Technician Series
Gs-2199 - Transportation Student Trainee Series

GS-2200 – INFORMATION TECHNOLOGY GROUP

Series in this group are:
GS-2210 - Information Technology Management Series
GS-2299 - Information Technology Student Trainee

The actual salary that the agency offers will be dependent on your qualifications. The general qualifications needed to receive that pay (and equivalent GS grade) is determined by the grade of the position. Please see the announcement for specific education and experience requirements for the position.

Salary Range (based on the 2010 pay schedule)	Qualifications Requirements
$20,000 – 35,600	High school with no experience (for GS-2) to one year of specialized experience at the GS-4 level, or four years of education beyond high school (for GS-5).
$27,400 – 44,000	Three years of general experience or one year of specialized experience or a bachelor's degree (for GS-5) or one year of graduate work or superior academic achievement as an undergraduate (for GS-7).
$40,000 – 65,400	Masters degree or equivalent or one year of specialized experience equal to GS-7 (for GS-9) or Ph.D. or equivalent or one year of specialized experience equal to GS-9 (for GS-11).
$60,000 – 129,500	One year of specialized experience equal to experience at the next lower grade (GS 12 through 15).

NOTE: In 2010, locality pay can increase the above ranges by 4.72 to 35.15 percent.

Qualifying Based on Education Alone

GS-2:   High school graduation or equivalent (i.e., GED)

GS-3:   One year above high school

GS-4:   Two years above high school (or Associate's degree)

GS-5:   Bachelor's degree

GS 7:   One full year of graduate study or Bachelor's degree with superior academic achievement (GPA 2.95 or higher out of a possible 4.0)

GS-9:   Master's degree or equivalent such as J.D. or LL.B.

GS-11:   Ph.D.

NOTE: There are exceptions to this chart; there are occupations that will not accept education in lieu of experience.

Military Rank to U.S. Federal Civilian Grades and Pay

You can use this chart below to estimate the federal grade equivalents for military rank. However, there is no one-to-one grade equivalent between the General Schedule and the military grading system. HR specialists rate applications based on the experience described in your resume. It is, therefore, important to describe your experience to a degree of detail that clearly portrays the level of responsibilities you had, the complexity of your work, the supervision you received, the guidelines you followed, and the impact of your work. Also, remember that volunteer work for which you received little or no pay is given the same credit as comparable paid experience.

Federal Civilian Grade—General Schedule	Federal Civilian Grade—Wage System	Military—Commissioned Officer (Army/Air Force/ UMSC, then Navy/Coast Guard ranks)	Military—Warrant Officer	Military--Enlisted
GS-01				E-1
GS-02				E-3
GS-03	WG 1-8			E-4
GS-04	WG 9-11			E-4
GS-05	WL 1-5			E-5
GS-06	WS 1-7			E-6
GS-07		O-1 Second Lieutenant or Ensign	WO-1	
GS-08				E-7
GS-09	WG 12-15	O-2 First Lieutenant or Lieutenant (Junior Grade)	CWO-2	
GS-10	WS 8-13			E-8
	WL 6-14			
GS-11		O-3 Captain or Lieutenant	CWO-3	E-9
GS-12		O-4 Major or Lieutenant Commander	CWO-4	
GS-13	WS 14-19	O-4 or 5 Lieutenant Colonel/Major or Commander/Lieutenant Commander	CWO-5	
GS-14	WL-15	O-5 Lieutenant Colonel or Commander		
GS-15		O-6 Colonel or Captain		
SES or equivalent		O-7 Brigadier General or Rear Admiral (Lower Half) O-8 Major General or Rear Admiral (Upper Half) O-9 Lieutenant General or Vice Admiral O-10 General or Admiral		

Effective January 2010 – Annual Rates by Grade and Step

www.opm.gov/oca/09tables/html/gs.asp

Grade	Step 1	Step 2	Step 3	Step 4	Step 5	Step 6	Step 7	Step 8	Step 9	Step 10	WIthin Grade
1	17803	18398	18990	19579	20171	20519	21104	21694	21717	22269	VARIES
2	20017	20493	21155	21717	21961	22607	23253	23899	24545	25191	VARIES
3	21840	22568	23296	24024	24752	25480	26208	26936	27664	28392	728
4	24518	25335	26152	26969	27786	28603	29420	30237	31054	31871	817
5	27431	28345	29259	30173	31087	32001	32915	33829	34743	35657	914
6	30577	31596	32615	33634	34653	35672	36691	37710	38729	39748	1019
7	33979	35112	36245	37378	38511	39644	40777	41910	43043	44176	1133
8	37631	38885	40139	41393	42647	43901	45155	46409	47663	48917	1254
9	41563	42948	44333	45718	47103	48488	49873	51258	52643	54028	1385
10	45771	47297	48823	50349	51875	53401	54927	56453	57979	59505	1526
11	50287	51963	53639	55315	56991	58667	60343	62019	63695	65371	1676
12	60274	62283	64292	66301	68310	70319	72328	74337	76346	78355	2009
13	71674	74063	76452	78841	81230	83619	86008	88397	90786	93175	2389
14	84697	87520	90343	93166	95989	98812	101635	104458	107281	110104	2823
15	99628	102949	106270	109591	112912	116233	119554	122875	126196	129517	3321

Now that we have covered the basic general schedule grade and pay system, we'll tell you that not every agency follows this pay system anymore. "Pay banding," which allows an organization to combine two or more grades into a wider "band" is an increasingly popular alternate to the traditional GS system. The "grade" information for jobs in agencies using pay banding will have a different look, and that look may be specific to a particular agency. Don't be surprised to see something as odd as ZP-1 or NO-2 in place of GS-5 or GS-7. Focus on the duties, the salary, whether you are qualified for the job, and whether you would like to have it. Remember, the federal government is large, and needs a way to increase flexibility of pay based on performance. Pay bands are its answer.

Examples of Pay Band Salaries

Department of Commerce, National Institute of Standards and Technology Pay Bands

	GS 1	GS 2	GS 3	GS 4	GS 5	GS 6	GS 7	GS 8	GS 9	GS 10	GS 11	GS 12	GS 13	GS 14	GS 15
ZA Administrative			1					2			3			4	5
ZP Professional			1					2			3			4	5
ZS Support	1	2		3		4			5						
ZT Technical		1				2				3		4	5		

Navy Research Lab

	GS 1	GS 2	GS 3	GS 4	GS 5	GS 6	GS 7	GS 8	GS 9	GS 10	GS 11	GS 12	GS 13	GS 14	GS 15	GS 16+
NP Scientist & Engineer Professional		I					II					III		IV		V
NR Scientist & Engineer Technical		I				II			III		IV	V				
NO Administrative Specialist/Professional		I					II					III	IV	V		
NC Administrative Support		I				II		III								

The human resources staffing specialist will detemine your qualifications for the position by looking at the following items in your federal resume. Qualification determinations are based on:

EDUCATION

- ➢ Major field of study
- ➢ # of years completed or # of semester hours completed
- ➢ GPA

TRAINING

- ➢ Related to job
- ➢ # of days or hours

EXPERIENCE

- ➢ Quality of experience
  - • Directly related to the job or general nature of work
  - • Complexity of assignments (what, for whom, why)
  - • Decision-making authority or span of control
  - • Knowledge, skills, and abilities used
- ➢ Length of experience
  - • Full-time or part-time
  - • # of hours per week

PATCO

Federal jobs are made up of the following basic categories, titles, and grades:

Professional – GS-5 through 15

Professional positions, such as chemists, accountants, doctors, social workers, and psychologists, have a positive educational requirement. They must be educated and certified by a board or institution.

Administrative – GS-5 through 15

These jobs usually have the title of Analyst or Specialist. Administrative jobs do not require a degree. You can qualify for an Administrative (Analyst or Specialist) position based on specialized experience, education, or both. Certain law enforcement positions are in this category: Special Agent, Border Patrol, Customs Inspector, Immigration Inspector.

Technical – GS-6 through 12

These jobs are the Technician or Assistant positions. Some job titles are Accounting Technicians or Assistants. There is no educational requirement. The main requirement is experience. The Federal Aviation Administration Electronics Technician can be classified as high as a GS-12. Bachelor's degree graduates can qualify for Technician or Assistant positions starting at GS-7 with superior academic achievement.

Clerical – GS-1 through 5

These jobs are Clerk positions. There is no educational requirement.
An Associate of Arts degree graduate will qualify for GS-3 or GS-4 position.

Other

Law enforcement professionals (not special agents), including security guards, police, rangers, park rangers, and U.S. Marshals; blue collar and other professions not covered in other categories.

The different classes of jobs in the federal government each have different hiring practices. This information is important for you to strategize your application depending on the job type you are applying for.

Competitive Service Jobs

Competitive Service jobs are under U.S. Office of Personnel Management's (OPM) jurisdiction and follow laws to ensure that applicants and employees receive fair and equal treatment in the hiring process. Selecting officials have broad authority to review more than one applicant source before determining the best-qualified candidate based on job-related criteria. Positions are open to the public. For positions lasting more than 120 days, vacancies must be announced and posted on USAJOBS, the federal government's central repository of job information. Veterans' preference rules are applied. Candidates are ranked and referred in order, i.e., highest scoring candidates or candidates in the highest quality group are referred first for selection. However, compensable disabled veterans "float" to the top, except for scientific and professional upper-level positions.

Excepted Service Jobs

Excepted Service jobs are the jobs with agencies that set their own qualification requirements and are not subject to the appointment, pay, and classification rules in Title 5, United States Code. These agencies are able to be more flexible with recruitment incentives, salaries, promotions, and other personnel matters. They are also subject to veterans' preference. Positions may be in the excepted service by law, executive order, or action of OPM. Excepted service jobs are not required to be posted on USAJOBS. To learn about their job opportunities, you must go to the specific agency websites.

Direct Hire

Agencies use direct hiring when there is a shortage of qualified candidates, or when an agency has a critical hiring need, such as one caused by an emergency or unanticipated events, or changed mission requirements. Direct hire provides a quick way to hire individuals in the competitive service. Although it requires agencies to publicly post their vacancies on USAJOBS, they do not need to apply veterans' preference or rate and rank qualified candidates. Once a qualified candidate is found, agencies may offer the job on the spot and may appoint the candidate immediately. OPM has allowed government-wide use of direct hire for the following occupations: information technology management related to security; x-ray technicians; medical officers, nurses, and pharmacists; and positions involved in Iraqi reconstruction efforts requiring fluency in Arabic.

Federal Career Intern Program (FCIP)

The Federal Career Intern Program is designed to help agencies recruit and attract exceptional individuals into a variety of occupations. This program is NOT intended for students only. Anyone can apply. In general, individuals are appointed to a two-year excepted service internship. Upon successful completion of the internships, the interns may be eligible for permanent placement within an agency. It is intended for positions at grade levels GS-5, 7, and 9. This program requires agencies to train and develop the interns. Individuals interested in FCIP opportunities must contact specific agencies directly. FCIP vacancies are not required to be posted on USAJOBS. The applicant must meet OPM's qualification requirements in order to be hired, and veterans' preference rules apply.

QUALIFICATIONS ANALYSIS

The following questions and answers will provide information concerning any special hiring programs that can offer you faster job consideration

GENERAL INFORMATION
Name:
U.S. Citizen? Yes No
Email where you would like to receive your narrative report:
Home phone:
Work phone:

VETERANS QUESTIONS
Read more details about various veteran's federal job benefits here: www.opm.gov/veterans
Were you in the military service? Yes No
If so, what branch of the service and your highest rank:

Do you know what your Preference is?
Points for Preference:
Period of Military Service:
Retired Military?

SECURITY CLEARANCE
Do you have a clearance?
Have you ever had a clearance? Yes No
If yes, what were the dates?
What type of clearance?

LANGUAGE SKILLS
Do you speak any foreign languages?
Yes No
If so, what:
Is your skill level? Fair, Moderate, Fluent

FOREIGN RESIDENCE / EMPLOYMENT
Have you lived overseas? If so, when and why?
Briefly answer this:

COMPUTER SKILLS
What is your level with computer skills?
Personal use, system development, advanced, professional?

FEDERAL AGENCY PREFERENCE
Do you have an agency preference, if you had your choice?
Write your answers here:

PAST FEDERAL EMPLOYMENT?
If you ever held a federal position:
Federal Civilian Pay Plan, Series, Grade, and months held:

SALARY EXPECTATIONS?
LOWEST SALARY you will accept?

WHAT ARE YOUR JOB TITLES?

List job titles of positions for which you wish to be considered. For instance: business manager, marketing director, customer services, etc.

FEDERAL EMPLOYMENT STATUS QUESTIONS

The federal government gives certain people preference (or status) for hiring if they are among these groups:

Are you married to a person in the military?

Are you disabled?

Have you worked for the federal government? If so, are you eligible to be reinstated without competition?

Are you eligible for placement in the federal service based upon your former military service? (i.e. are you eligible for a Veterans Recruitment Appointment?)

EDUCATION

Do you have a degree? If so, what was your major? Graduation date?

Have you just graduated with a 3.5 GPA?

If you do not have a degree yet, what have you been studying?

CERTIFICATION

Do you have any special certifications?

SKILLS

What are your five most significant skills? (computer, writing, speaking, research, etc.)

KNOWLEDGE

What types of knowledge do you have? (real estate, administrative, business, etc.)

INTERESTS

What types of positions interest you? (administration, contracts, finance, accounting, IT, engineering, etc.)

Why Network?

The U.S. federal government employs nearly two million people in civilian jobs, making it the biggest employer in the country. Understandably, the hiring system can sometimes be complex and daunting. Networking is a great opportunity to learn about the federal hiring system. Other people, especially current and former federal employees, are often the best source of basic information and insider tips.

Who Do You Know and Why is it Important?

Do you know a supervisor at an agency or a military base? It's possible that veterans could get hired by this supervisor. The Veterans Recruitment Act (VRA) offers special hiring programs for retiring and separating military (disabled or non-disabled). VRA gives supervisors the authority to make direct hires in the case of veterans, but even under direct hiring, the jobseeker must submit an application.

Contact List
Make a list of federal employee contacts and keep their information handy for networking.

Name of person:

Agency where he/she works:

Location:

Job title:

What does he or she do in the government?

The best opportunity for a direct hire is a military job fair. Job fairs are held frequently. On occasion, the federal human resources specialists will bring along actual positions in the government. If you can find a military job fair where agencies are present, it is very possible that you could be given a job offer on the spot! Of course, your chances increase astronomically if you are well-prepared. Take the time to understand federal employment, how to qualify, how to write a federal resume, and how to present your skills professionally. Have your resume ready to hand out. Also, practice the job fair script before you go.

Job Fair Script
Prepare your own job fair script here. Practice your script with a friend.

Hello, my name is: _____

Where are you from? _____

Your job before military service: _____

Military service: _____
_____

Recent activity: _____
What was involved in that? _____
What was the result of that activity? _____
What was your role? _____

What kind of job are you looking for? _____
_____
_____

What are your basic skills? _____
_____
_____

Where do you want to live now? _____
_____
_____

JOHN W. SMITH

Walter Reed Army Medical Center
Malogne House Bldg.20, Room 181
6900 Georgia Ave., NW
Washington, DC 20307
Phone: (202) 888-8888
Citizenship: United States of America

Permanent Address:
120 CR 546
Ripley, MS 21228
email: johnsmith@yahoo.com

Veterans' Preference: 10-point, E-4, Mississippi Army National Guard, 2001 to present, Recipient of Purple Heart

SKILLS AND JOB OBJECTIVES:

Team Leader
Law Enforcement
Special Projects

Veteran's Benefits Counselor and Advocate
Emergency Management Coordination
Communications

PROFESSIONAL EXPERIENCE:

Intern, Congressman Gene Taylor – 4th Congressional District of Mississippi
2311 Rayburn House Office Building
Washington, DC 20515-2405
Supervisor: Harry Hoffman (202) 222-5555

August 2005 - Present
Salary: N/A
Supervisor may be contacted

While recuperating and completing physical therapy for injuries sustained as an escort Military Policeman in Iraqi Freedom, served as an Intern for Congressman Gene Taylor.

- ADMINISTRATIVE ASSISTANT: Tasks included word processing, managing files and records, producing reports, designing forms, and other office procedures. Researched and produced reports on veteran's benefits activities. Corresponded with veterans.

- CONSTITUENT SERVICES: Provided customer and personal services to veterans concerning benefits and programs following injuries.

- VETERANS' BENEFITS RESEARCH: Researched TRICARE health insurance issues for national guardsmen and reservists while not on active duty. Advocated for veterans' benefits and provided information to representatives of the Department of Veterans' Affairs. Wrote summaries of veterans' problems and situations concerning processes and service treatment while being transferred from Walter Reed Army Medical Center to outlying regional centers.

JOHN W. SMITH, page two

Accomplishments:

- **Hurricane Katrina / Veterans Home Coordinator**: Coordinated the relocation of 300+ veterans from the Armed Forces Retirement Home in Gulfport, Mississippi to the U.S. Soldiers' and Airmen's Home located in Washington DC during the aftermath of Hurricane Katrina. Established phone card and clothing drives to ensure that each veteran had sufficient clothing and was able to contact family and friends concerning their whereabouts. <u>Awarded the Humanitarian Service Medal and the Mississippi Emergency Service Medal for my actions</u>.

Military Police, Mississippi Army National Guard

155th Separate Armored Brigade   July 2003 - Present
2924 HWY 51 South, Canton, MS 21042   Salary: $21,000/year
Supervisor: Capt. Stephen McCarthy (333) 888-8888   Supervisor may be contacted

- LEAD MILITARY PATROL AND LAW ENFORCEMENT: Lead military police patrol. Coordinate compound and work projects, preserve military control.
- TRAINER AND COORDINATOR: Train law enforcement personnel.
- TRAFFIC ACCIDENT INVESTIGATOR
- PHYSICAL SECURITY
- CIVIL DISTURBANCE AND RIOT CONTROL OPERATIONS

Manufacturing/Operations/Production

Ashley Furniture Factory   2002 - 2004
15900 State Highway 15 North, Ripley, MS 38663

- MANUFACTURING OPERATIONS MANAGEMENT
- CUSTOMER SERVICE AND PROBLEM-SOLVING

Equipment Operator/Supervisor

Pressmen Impact, Inc., New Haven, MS   1995 - 2003

- SUPERVISOR IN GOVERNMENT CONTRACTOR MANUFACTURING FIRM: Supervised custom impact extrusions serving aviation and military needs.
- TRAINED EQUIPMENT OPERATORS in safety and operations.
- EQUIPMENT OPERATIONS: Operated vehicles, forklifts and heavy machinery.

EDUCATION: Rydell High School, Rydell, Mississippi 37771, Graduated 1991
Mississippi Community College, Boonsboro, MS 38882
Major: Criminal Justice and Social Work, Semester Hours: 56 hours

LICENSE: Commercial Drivers License (Class A)

AWARDS: Army Commendation Medal, Iraq Campaign Medal, Global War on Terrorism, Expeditionary Medal, Purple Heart, Humanitarian Service Medal, Mississippi Emergency Service Medal, National Defense Service Medal, Army Service Ribbon, Armed Forces Reserve Medal

Anna S. Ward

1347 Elliott Way / Annapolis, MD 21225
Cellular: 410-444-4444 / Residence: 410-444-4444
Email: asward@aol.com

Eligible: Noncompetitive Appointment of Certain Military Spouses, 5 CFR Parts 315 and 316
Veterans Preference: None
[or]
Veterans preference: 10-points derived preference

PROFILE:

- Over 5 years of administrative, training and customer service experience.
- Excellent communications skills with demonstrated writing and public speaking expertise.
- Proven interpersonal skills; able to successfully negotiate and build coalitions between groups with opposing or disparate objectives.
- Strong commitment to organizational goals and improving operations and customer service.
- Detail-oriented, able to identify, research and correct discrepancies.

WORK EXPERIENCE

Direct Placement Recruiter, Adecco Direct Placement
Baltimore, MD   08/2005 – present

Recruiting: Utilize multiple recruiting techniques including internet sourcing, cold-calling.
Customer Service / Client Relations: In-depth questioning when taking job orders.
Human Resources: Assist client companies in review and revision of position descriptions.
Training: Coach candidates on job search and interview topics.
Sales / Marketing: Present prospective clients with broad spectrum of information.
Administration: Use of interactive database to track candidate information.

Key Accomplishment: Designed and implemented six-week blitz marketing campaign using pre-printed flyers and brochures, phone calls and personal notes to reach hiring authorities within target businesses. Tracked marketing campaign results for analysis.

Assistant Program Coordinator, Innovative Management, Inc.
Henderson Hall, USMC, Arlington, VA   01/2005 – 06/2005

Government Contractor / Assistant Coordinator of Volunteer Programs for Henderson Hall, Headquarters Battalion, Headquarters Marine Corps.
RECRUITING / RESOURCE MANAGEMENT: Recruited active duty, retiree and military personnel.

Director Of First Impressions (Reception), Fotoball Usa, Inc.
San Diego, CA   09/2002 – 05/2003

Fotoball USA, Inc is a premier sports and entertainment marketer and manufacturer.
Administrative / Customer Service: Responded to all inquiries.
Award: Received Outstanding Performance "Whatever It Takes" Award, 12/2002.

Family Advocacy Administrative Assistant, GS-0303-03, United States Marine Corps, Student Temporary Employment Program

Marine Corps Recruit Depot, San Diego, CA   12/2001 – 07/2002

Administrative: Support for program manager, two counselors and one victim advocate.

Career Transition Workshop Facilitator, Native American Management Services (NAMS)

Mclean, VA   08/2001 – 06/2003

Training: Facilitated two and three-day workshops to groups of 5 to 60 transitioning personnel.

Management Assistance Corporation, Volunteer Program Coordinator Assistant, Henderson Hall

Fairfax, VA   04/2000 – 07/2001

Recruited volunteers for both military and civilian agencies and events.

EDUCATION

- Graduate Coursework, Juris Doctorate, Catholic University of America, Columbus School of Law, Washington, DC; 2004-2005. 15 credits.
- Bachelor of Science, Behavioral and Social Science, University of Maryland University College, Adelphi, MD, 2003; GPA: 3.8; Worked full and part-time throughout BS Degree studies.

COMPUTER AND OFFICE MACHINE PROFICIENCIES

- MS Office: Word, Excel, Outlook, Access, PowerPoint; copiers, fax machines, printers, multi-line phone systems Typing: 45+ WPM

AWARDS / RECOGNITION

Certificate of Appreciation, Major General Huly, USMC, "for substantial contributions...." as Administrative Assistant. 08/2002
Leadership Education Seminar (presenter) MCAS Miramar, 05/2002
Certificate of Appreciation, Outstanding Volunteer Service, MCAS Miramar, 04/2002

COMMUNITY SERVICE AND INTERESTS

Partnerships in Education, MCAS Miramar, California:

Volunteered to coordinate and schedule events at Miramar for San Diego City Schools Partnerships in Education program. These partnerships promoted student achievement by learning about MCAS purpose and mission through job-shadowing and assisting with Reserve Officer Training Corps activities.

On average, there are 20,000 jobs listed everyday. The best way to understand where you fit in government is to go searching for jobs that fit your experience and interests. Federal vacancy announcements (job advertisements) contain all of the information you need to compare your background to the position requirements.

Learn how to read job announcements

For instance, when you read the **agency name and office** of the job, you will automatically know the mission of the agency and the customers they serve. The job title can reflect the purpose of the job, or the title might be generic. If the job title is Program Analyst, you would need to read the Duties section of the position to determine if this job is right for you.

The **Qualifications** section details the experience necessary for the job. It could say: three years specialized experience. If you don't have this specialized experience, then this job is not a good fit for you. Some announcements include a list of Questions or Knowledge, Skills, and Abilities (KSAs). These can help you further determine if you qualify for the job.

Find job announcements
Learn how to search USAJOBS. Best search system:
1. Geographic area preference
2. Salary/grade level
3. All Agencies
4. All jobs in this area
5. YES (for Merit Promotion positions)

Follow the Directions!

The following items are the most important elements of a vacancy announcement. Be sure to study each of these items on every announcement so that you follow the directions successfully.

Title of Job and Grade and Geographic Location

Make sure it's correct for you.

Closing Date

If announcement reads: "Open Continuously," "Inventory Building," or has a date that is two years away, then this announcement is a database-building announcement. If the announcement has specific open and close dates, check if your application has to be received or postmarked by the closing date. If the announcement has already closed, but you are a compensably disabled veteran, call the HR office and ask how you can submit your late application. If you are applying online in a resume builder, try to apply one day early in case there are complications.

Who Can Apply

This is very important. You should only apply to positions where you can qualify. You will see the following notes in this sections:

- Open to Anyone

- All US Citizens

- Status Only (this means current federal employees, reinstatement federal employees, veterans, spouses with noncompetitive applicants, or persons with disabilities)

Location/Duty Station

Make sure you are willing to work in this geographic location. Check the announcement to see if people can apply who live outside the geographic region of the position.

Knowledge, Skills, and Abilities

Read the announcement to see if they list KSAs. They are to be eliminated in the near future, so, if KSAs are listed, you might include them in the federal resume instead of on separate sheets of paper.

Questionnaires

Check to see if the announcement requires completion of a questionnaire. In these "assessment questionnaires," you choose your level of skill and experience for each question. You may need to provide examples to demonstrate your experience.

Duties

The description of duties will be written based on the actual position description. The write-up will include "keywords" that should be included in a federal resume.

Qualifications

Are you qualified? Read the qualifications to determine if you have the general and specialized qualifications. If the announcement states one year, that means 52 weeks, 40 hours per week.

General experience is experience that will demonstrate your ability to acquire the particular knowledge and skills for the job. Qualifying general experience will vary in its degree of specificity from one job to another. For some, any progressively responsible work experience may be qualifying. Others may require experience that provided a familiarity with the subject matter or processes of the job. For example, an entry level accounting technician position may require general experience that provided a basic knowledge of debit and credit.

Specialized experience is typically required for positions above the entry level where applicants must have demonstrated that they possess the ability to perform successfully the duties of a position after a normal orientation period. Specialized experience is typically in or related to the work of the postion to be filled. For example, to meet the specialized experience requirements for an accounting technican responsible for maintaining accounts receivables, the applicant would likely be required to have a specific level of experience performing duties such as sending monthly bills, receiving payments, and maintaining accounts receivable ledgers.

How to Apply

Carefully read the "how to apply" instructions as they will differ from agency to agency. The usual application includes a resume, KSAs (maybe), last performance evaluation (if possible), DD-214 (if you were in the military), and transcripts (sometimes, not often).

SPECIALIZED EXPERIENCE

is usually defined as "one year specialized experience" that is similar to the position in the announcement. This section of an announcement is very important for federal resume writers. The announcement will often say, "Examples include" then suggest examples. Your federal resume MUST cover this specialized experience somewhere in the work experience. Your example does NOT have to be the most recent position; it can be from any point in your work history, but preferably from the last 10 years.

⌐ **Search Jobs**   ⌐ **My Account**   ⌐ **Info Center**   **Welcome KATHRYN! | Sign out**

USAJOBS®
"WORKING FOR AMERICA"

Search Jobs Keyword Tips ?
What: (keywords)   Where: (city, state or zip code) ▶
Browse Jobs >   Advanced/International Search >

< **Back to Results** | **OVERVIEW** | **DUTIES** | **QUALIFICATIONS & EVALUATIONS** | **BENEFITS & OTHER INFO** | **HOW TO APPLY**

Army Installation Management Agency

Job Title: Facility Services Assistant
Department: Department Of The Army
Agency: Army Installation Management Command
Job Announcement Number: SWDM10196426D

SALARY RANGE:	38,790.00 - 50,431.00 USD /year
OPEN PERIOD:	Thursday, May 13, 2010 to Monday, May 24, 2010
SERIES & GRADE:	GS-1603-07/07
POSITION INFORMATION:	-This is a Permanent position. -- Full Time
DUTY LOCATIONS:	1 vacancy - KY - Ft. Knox
WHO MAY BE CONSIDERED:	US Citizens

JOB SUMMARY:
Challenge Yourself - Be an Army Civilian - Go Army!

Civilian employees serve a vital role in supporting the Army mission. They provide the skills that are not readily available in the military, but crucial to support military operations. The Army integrates the talents and skills of its military and civilian members to form a Total Army.

Organization(s):
US Army Installation Management Command, DPTMS, Training Division, Fort Knox, KY 40121

About the Position: Selectee serves as the facility manager receiving general guidance from the Operations and Plans Manager for the Fort Knox Battle Command Training Facilities. Facility consists of classrooms, Administrative and Instructor Offices, four open bay areas for virtual and constructive simulation training, two Conference Rooms, two Break Areas, numerous storage areas, the surrounding grounds and parking areas. Selectee serves as Primary Hand Receipt Holder for all Battle Command Training Branch (BCTB) equipment, and may also serve as an Assistant Instructor in the BCTB for some Army Battle Command Systems.
Who May Apply: Click here for more information.
● All U. S. citizens.

KEY REQUIREMENTS:

● U.S. Citizen

Apply Online ▶
Print Preview ▶
Save Job ▶
Share Job ▶

Agency Information:
Central Resume Processing Center
314 Johnson Street
Aberdeen Proving Ground, MD
21005-5283

Questions about this job:
Central Resume Processing Center
Phone: 410-306-0137
Email:
applicanthelp@cpsrxtp.belvoir.army.mil

Job Announcement Number:
SWDM10196426D
Control Number: 1908522

> This is a permanent position, but be sure to check that you will accept temp and term positions in your USAJOBS profile.

> Check out the mission to see if there are keywords you can use.

Duties

Back to top ▲

Additional Duty Location Info:

1 vacancy - Frederick county (Ft Detrick area), MD

> The Duties Section contains keywords for the Outline Format federal resume.

Maintain the Facility Management Software System (FMSS), database in order to support park regional and departmental goals for reporting accurate and pertinent information to park assets, maintenance, and construction requirements, expenditures, and accomplishments.

Retrieve data, prepare and present reports to management from FMSS, the Facility condition Assessment System (FCAS), and the Cost Estimating Software System (CESS) databases for operational and fiscal purposes.

Provide information to support the agency's Government Performance and Results Act (GPRA) goals related to asset management.

Ensure that accurate and timely records/data are entered in the the FMSS/FCAS databases.

Qualifications and Evaluations

Back to top ▲

QUALIFICATIONS REQUIRED:

> Review the Qualifications for more keywords for your resume and cover letter.

In order to qualify for this position you must meet the following by the closing date of the vacancy announcement:

Qualifications for GS-05: You must have one year of specialized experience equivalent to at least the GS-4 level in the Federal service. Your resume must demonstrate that you clearly possess experience/knowledge sufficient to perform duties such as a working knowledge in operating facility management computer programs, assisting in the preparation/execution of data entry; using various word processing, database and spreadsheet software.

Education Requirement for GS 05

Successful completion of at least four years above high school education in any field for which high school graduation or the equivalent is the normal prerequisite.

OR

A combination of specialized experience as described in A above and education as described in B above which total at least one year. For example, 6 months of specialized experience (50% of the experience) and 9 graduate level semester hours (50% of the education), would qualify an applicant for this position.

If you are qualifying based on education, please submit a copy of your college transcript so that we can verify your coursework. It need not be an official transcript; however, if you are selected, you may be required to submit an official transcript prior to entering on duty.

Education completed in foreign colleges or universities may be used to meet the above requirements if you can show that the foreign education is comparable to that received in an accredited educational institution in the United States. It is your responsibility to provide such evidence when applying.

Qualifications for GS-06: You must have one year of specialized experience equivalent to at least the GS-5 level in the Federal service. Your resume must demonstrate that you clearly possess experience/knowledge sufficient to perform duties such as assisting in the preparation/execution of data entry; using various word processing, database and spreadsheet software, office automation and administrative functions, and maintenance budgeting processes.

Qualifications for GS-07: You must have one year of specialized experience equivalent to at least the GS-6 level in the Federal service. Your resume must demonstrate that you clearly possess experience/knowledge sufficient to perform duties such as establishing standing work orders in an organization, using database and spreadsheet software, maintenance and budgeting processes, construction and facility maintenance concepts establishing standing work orders, supplies, materials, and equipment needed to complete the identified work; input data such as the organization's hierarchy of locations, assets, equipment inventory, vendors, budget and account information into a program data base and independently verify the accuracy of this information; generate inspection documents for all organizational assets; prepare cost estimates for asset deficiencies, or similar administrative duties.

> Make sure to cover the "One Year Specialized Experience" requirements in your resume.

Requirements

 Appointment will be subject to a pre-employment background investigation. Under the requirements of the Homeland Security Presidential Directive 12 (HSPD-12), all new Federal Employees must pass a background investigation. Failure to successfully meet these requirements will be grounds for termination.

New employees of the Department of the Interior must identify a financial institution for direct deposit of net pay within 30 day of entrance on duty.

NPS uniformed position. Employee will be required to wear a uniform and comply with National Park Service uniform standards.

This is not a drug tested position.

HOW YOU WILL BE EVALUATED:

A review of your application will be made to ensure you meet the basic job requirements. In addition, we will evaluate your responses to the attached online Assessment Questionnaire to measure the degree to which your background matches the requirements for the position.

To determine if you are qualified for this job, a review of your resume, supporting documentation, and responses to the Assessment Questionnaire will be conducted. If, after reviewing your resume and/or supporting documentation, a determination is made that you have inflated your qualifications and/or experience, your score may be adjusted to more accurately reflect your competencies.

The Assessment Questionnaire is designed to measure your ability in the following competencies needed to successfully perform on the job:

- Information Management

- Computer Operation

- Oral and Written Communication

Back to top ▲

Benefits and Other Info

BENEFITS:

The Federal Government offers a comprehensive benefits package. Explore the major benefits offered to most Federal employees at http://www.usajobs.gov/EI/benefits.asp#icc

Annual and Sick Leave: Most Federal employees earn both annual and sick leave. For additional information visit: http:www.opmlgov/oca/leave/index.asp

OTHER INFORMATION:

Career Transition Assistance Program (CTAP)/ Interagency Career Transition Assistance Program (ICTAP): To be well-qualified and exercise selection priority for this vacancy, displaced Federal employees must be rated at 85 or above on the rating criteria for this position. CTAP/ICTAP eligibles must submit one of the following as proof of eligibility for the special selection priority: A separation notice; a "Notice of Personnel Action" (SF-50) documenting separation; an agency certification that you cannot be placed after injury compensation has been terminated; an OPM notification that your disability annuity has been terminated; OR a Military Department or National Guard Bureau notification that are retired under 5 U.S.C. 8337(h) or 8456. For additional information on how to apply as an ICTAP eligible see http://www.opm.gov/rif/employee_guides/career_transition.asp#ictap.

Special Appointment Authority: Individuals who are eligible for consideration under a special hiring authority (i.e., 30% compensable veterans, VRA eligibles, severely disabled individuals, former Peace Corps and VISTA volunteers, etc.) will be accepted and considered non-competitively for this vacancy. Special hiring authority eligibles must indicate on their application if they are applying under a special program and submit proof of eligibility with their application. The VRA hiring authority is limited to positions at the GS-11 level and below.

Travel, transportation and relocation expenses **will be paid** if the person selected for the position is from outside the local commuting area and is otherwise eligible for reimbursement of relocation expenses under the Federal Travel Regulations.

> This announcement is a USAJOBS / Application Manager combo application.

> Assessment Questionnaire could contain keywords.

> These competencies are keywords for your resume.

> Includes spouse and family member programs.

> Travel and relocation expenses are covered. Excellent!

How To Apply

Back to top ▲

HOW TO APPLY:

To begin click the *Apply Online* button and follow the prompts to register and submit all required documents and complete the assessment questionnaire.

To return to your saved application, log in to your USAJOBS account at www.usajobs.opm.gov and click on "Application Status". Click on the position title, and then select **Apply Online** to continue.

We strongly encourage you to apply online. If you cannot apply online, you may FAX your resume, assessment questionnaire, and supporting documents to (478) 757-3144. You must print a copy of OPM Form 1203-FX, document your responses to the assessment questionnaire View Occupational Questionnaire and use the official FAX coversheet found here.

> *Make sure to use this fax cover if you are sending documents via fax.*

REQUIRED DOCUMENTS:

- Resume showing relevant experience (cover letter optional)

- Veterans' Preference Documentation (DD-214, VA Letter, and SF-15 if claiming 10-point Veterans' Preference; DD-214 if claiming 5 point preference)

- SF-50 for proof of Merit Promotion eligibility, or documentation showing VEOA eligibility, if applicable.

- ICTAP/CTAP Documentation (see "Transition Assistance Plan" in online questionnaire) if applicable

> *Cover letter could be recommended in 11/2010.*

Documentation supporting eligibility for non-competitive appointment (e.g. severely disabled, eligible veterans, etc.), if applicable.

AGENCY CONTACT INFO:

Katina L. Harkless
Phone: (703)754-1652x1117
Email: katina_harkless@nps.gov

Agency Information:
WESTERN SERVICING HUMAN
RESOURCES OFFICE
PLEASE DO NOT MAIL OR
FAX APPS TO THIS ADDRESS
WASHINGTON, DC 20242

> *Also non-competitive spouse documents.*

WHAT TO EXPECT NEXT:

Once the online questionnaire is received you will receive an acknowledgement email that your submission was successful. After a review of your complete application is made you will be notified of your rating and/or referral to the hiring official. If further evaluation or interviews are required you will be contacted. After making a tentative job offer we will conduct a suitability and/or security background investigation.

Instructions for answering the questions in the Occupational Questionnaire: If you are applying to this announcement by completing the OPM 1203-FX form instead of using the Online Application method, please use the following step-by-step instructions as a guide to filling out the required questionnaire. You will need to print the vacancy announcement and refer to it as you answer the questions. You may omit any optional information; however, you must provide responses to all required questions. Be sure to double check your application before submission.

> *Watch for emails from HR.*

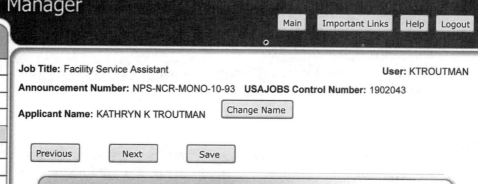

Application Manager

Main | Important Links | Help | Logout

Vacancy ID: 344024

Biographic Information
Eligibility Information
Other Information
Assessment Questionnaire
  Section 1
  Section 2
  Section 3
ReUse Documents
Upload Documents
Submit My Answers
View/Print My Answers

Job Title: Facility Service Assistant   **User:** KTROUTMAN

Announcement Number: NPS-NCR-MONO-10-93 **USAJOBS Control Number:** 1902043

Applicant Name: KATHRYN K TROUTMAN [Change Name]

[Previous]   [Next]   [Save]

Section 1   **Total Questions in this Assessment: 34**

From the descriptions below, select the one response that best describes how your background meets the specialized experience or education requirements for a Facility Services Assistant, GS-1603-05,06,07 position. Read all of the responses before making your selection. MARK ONLY ONE RESPONSE. If you select more than one response, or leave this question blank you will be rated ineligible. If you do not meet these minimum qualifications, you will be considered not qualified and will not receive consideration for this position.

THE RESUME OR APPLICATION MATERIALS YOU SUBMIT FOR THIS ANNOUNCEMENT MUST SUPPORT THE ANSWERS YOU CLAIM UNDER THIS AND OTHER QUESTIONS. IF NOT, YOU WILL BE FOUND NOT QUALIFIED OR YOUR SCORE WILL BE LOWERED.

1. Please select the response below which best describes your experience and/or education in relation to qualifying for the position of Facility Services Assistant at the GS-05.

  ○ **A** I have one year of specialized experience equivalent to at least the GS-4 level in the Federal service. My resume demonstrates that I clearly possess experience/knowledge sufficient to perform duties such as a working knowledge in operating facility management computer programs, assisting in the preparation/execution of data entry; using various word processing, database and spreadsheet software.

  ○ **B** I have successfully completed at least four years above high school education in any field for which high school graduation or the equivalent is the normal prerequisite. PLEASE NOTE: If you are using education to qualify, you must submit a copy of your college transcripts.

  ○ **C** I have a combination of specialized experience as described in A above and education as described in B above which total at least one year. For example, 6 months of specialized experience (50% of the experience) and 9 graduate level semester hours (50% of the education), would qualify an applicant for this position. PLEASE NOTE: If you are using education to qualify, you must submit a copy of your college transcripts.

  ○ **D** I do not have the experience or education as described above.

Besides specialized experience, education, and technical skills, what "value-added" competencies can you offer a supervisor?

What are competencies?
They are the characteristics affecting performance and are broader than the well-known KSAs (knowledge, skills, and abilities).

Examples

- Are you a team leader who listens to team members ideas, resolves problems quickly, strives to meet timelines, creates effective plans for training and execution, and gains cooperation and consensus during a project?

- Are you an IT specialist who, in addition to performing all the technical elements of the job, talks to customers about their IT problems, requests, and needs? Are you creative in coming up with solutions to problems?

- Are you an administrative professional who is customer-focused, follows up on inquiries, responds efficiently and effectively, and cares about the dilemmas that customers face?

Which agencies use core competencies?
The Veterans Administration, Office of Personnel Management, U.S. Marine Corps, Defense Finance & Accounting Service, and many other federal agencies are looking for qualified and skilled applicants, who are also skilled in certain core competencies.

How do I use core competencies for applying for jobs?
These characteristics go above and beyond skills. You can stand out in a government resume, question/essay narrative, or behavior-based interview by highlighting these competencies. Study this step and determine the top five or ten competencies that make you a stand-out employee in your field of work. Add these competencies to your resume in the work experience descriptions for a stronger federal resume!

VETERANS ADMINISTRATION CORE COMPETENCIES DESCRIPTIONS

Find your core competencies and check them off the list. Add a few of these competencies into the "duties" section of your work experience.

Interpersonal Effectiveness

❑ Builds and sustains positive relationships.
❑ Handles conflicts and negotiations effectively.
❑ Builds and sustains trust and respect.
❑ Collaborates and works well with others.
❑ Shows sensitivity and compassion for others.
❑ Encourages shared decision-making.
❑ Recognizes and uses ideas of others.
❑ Communicates clearly, both orally and in writing.
❑ Listens actively to others.
❑ Honors commitments and promises.

Customer Service

❑ Understands that customer service is essential to achieving our mission.
❑ Understands and meets the needs of internal customers.
❑ Manages customer complaints and concerns effectively and promptly.
❑ Designs work processes and systems that are responsive to customers.
❑ Ensures that daily work and the strategic direction is customer-centered.
❑ Uses customer feedback data in planning and providing products and services.
❑ Encourages and empowers subordinates to meet or exceed customer needs and expectations.
❑ Identifies and rewards behaviors that enhance customer satisfaction.

Flexibility/Adaptability

❑ Responds appropriately to new or changing situations.
❑ Handles multiple inputs and tasks simultaneously.
❑ Seeks and welcomes the ideas of others.
❑ Works well with all levels and types of people.
❑ Accommodates new situations and realities.
❑ Remains calm in high-pressure situations.
❑ Makes the most of limited resources.
❑ Demonstrates resilience in the face of setbacks.
❑ Understands change management.

Creative Thinking

- ❑ Appreciates new ideas and approaches.
- ❑ Thinks and acts innovatively.
- ❑ Looks beyond current reality and the "status quo".
- ❑ Demonstrates willingness to take risks.
- ❑ Challenges assumptions.
- ❑ Solves problems creatively.
- ❑ Demonstrates resourcefulness.
- ❑ Fosters creative thinking in others.
- ❑ Allows and encourages employees to take risks.
- ❑ Identifies opportunities for new projects and acts on them.
- ❑ Rewards risk-taking and non-successes and values what was learned.

Systems Thinking

- ❑ Understands the complexities of the agency and how the "product" is delivered.
- ❑ Appreciates the consequences of specific actions on other parts of the system.
- ❑ Thinks in context.
- ❑ Knows how one's role relates to others in the organization.
- ❑ Demonstrates awareness of the purpose, process, procedures, and outcomes of one's work.
- ❑ Encourages and rewards collaboration.

Organizational Stewardship

- ❑ Demonstrates commitment to people.
- ❑ Empowers and trusts others.
- ❑ Develops leadership skills and opportunities throughout organization.
- ❑ Develops team-based improvement processes.
- ❑ Promotes future-oriented system change.
- ❑ Supports and encourages lifelong learning throughout the organization.
- ❑ Manages physical, fiscal, and human resources to increase the value of products and services.
- ❑ Builds links between individuals and groups in the organization.
- ❑ Integrates organization into the community.
- ❑ Accepts accountability for self, others, and the organization's development.
- ❑ Works to accomplish the organizational business plan.

Technical Skills

- ❑ Displays knowledge and skills necessary to perform assigned duties.
- ❑ Understands processes, procedures, standards, methods, and technologies related to assignment.
- ❑ Demonstrates functional and technical literacy.
- ❑ Participates in measuring outcomes of work.
- ❑ Keeps current on new developments in field of expertise.
- ❑ Effectively uses available technology (voice mail, automation, software, etc.).

My core competencies are:

_____

_____

_____

_____

_____

_____

_____

_____

Office of Personnel Management, Senior Executive Service, Executive Core Qualifications

Leading Change	Leading People	Results Driven	Business Acumen	Building Coalitions
Definitions				
This core qualification involves the ability to bring about strategic change, both within and outside the organization, to meet organizational goals. Inherent to this ECQ is the ability to establish an organizational vision and to implement it in a continuously changing environment.	This core qualification involves the ability to lead people toward meeting the organization's vision, mission, and goals. Inherent to this ECQ is the ability to provide an inclusive workplace that fosters the development of others, facilitates cooperation and teamwork, and supports constructive resolution of conflicts.	This core qualification involves the ability to meet organizational goals and customer expectations. Inherent to this ECQ is the ability to make decisions that produce high-quality results by applying technical knowledge, analyzing problems, and calculating risks.	This core qualification involves the ability to manage human, financial, and information resources strategically.	This core qualification involves the ability to build coalitions internally and with other federal agencies, state and local governments, nonprofit and private sector organizations, foreign governments, or international organizations to achieve common goals.
Competencies				
Creativity and Innovation External Awareness Flexibility Resilience Strategic Thinking Vision	Conflict Management Leveraging Diversity Developing Others Team Building	Accountability Customer Service Decisiveness Entrepreneurship Problem Solving Technical Credibility	Financial Management Human Capital Management Technology Management	Partnering Political Savvy Influencing/ Negotiating

Marine Corps Core Competencies

Operations and Training Support

Goal 1: Support current and future deployment requirements.

Goal 2: Meet and anticipate Operating Forces' validated training requirements.

Goal 3: Shape land, sea and airspace training area on and off installation.

Goal 4: Support current and future Force Protection requirements.

Goal 5: Provide effective command and control.

Sustainment and Maintenance

Goal 6: Provide adequate facilities.

Goal 7: Environmental compliance.

Goal 8: Provide effective services.

Workforce Management

Goal 9: Achieve a viable and sustainable workforce.

Goal 10: Effectively manage military workforce.

Goal 11: Reduce safety mishaps.

> Compare Marine Corps Core Competencies
> with VA Core Competencies to understand
> the culture of each agency.

Keywords are just what they sound like: words that the human resources specialist or online builders are scanning for in your resume to see if you are a match. If your resume does not have certain keywords in it, your chances of getting your resume noticed are much less.

Where do I find keywords?

The DUTIES, SPECIALIZED EXPERIENCE, AND QUALIFICATIONS sections in the announcement contain the keywords you need for your resume. See this example below with the keywords bolded. Include the keywords in the resume if applicable.

Criminal Investigator, Peace Corps, GS 9-12 range, $40 - $77K

Announcement Duties Language:

- Performs work related to **developing and maintaining relationships** within and outside the agency to **communicate and disseminate information** about program mission and activities.
- Plans and **conducts criminal investigations** related to alleged or suspected violations of laws, regulations, and policies. Uses a variety of investigative techniques, such as **analyzing evidence**, collecting evidence, **conducting interviews**, **interrogating suspects**, collecting testimony, performing **undercover work**, maintaining **surveillance**, and **preparing reports**.

How do I get started?

Find two to five target vacancy announcements. Analyze the Duties, Qualifications, and Specialized Experience sections for keywords. Make a list of keywords and build your content from target jobs. Once you have drafted a basic resume, you can MATCH this resume to specific job announcements by including keywords from that job announcement in your resume.

LOGISTICS MANAGEMENT SPECIALIST, GS 12–15

Ability to Plan
Acctg Discrepancy
Accurate
Achieves Goals
Admin Functions
Aircraft
AIS
Am Soc Train & Dev
Analytical
Apparel
Armament
Arms Monitoring
Asn Supv & Curr Dev
Authorization Doc
Auto Data Process'g
Automotive Exp
Awards
Bachelors
Battle
Billeting
Budget
Budget Estimate
Budget Plan/Forecst
Budget Terms
C&E
Call Detail Record
Civ Per Mgmt
Clothing & Textil
Coach MentorMotiv
Comm
Comm Skill
Command
Communicat'n Skills
Community Center
Community Exp
Computr Tec
Conflict
Conflict Resolutn
Construction Work
Contact Person
COSIS
Course Development
Creative Writing
Crime
Crime Prevention

Cust Rel Mgmt
Customer Service
Customer Support
Damage Analysis
Data Analysis
Data Collection
Data Processing
Depreciation
Dept Housing
Design
Develop Briefing
Development
Dir Engineer
Distribution
Document Prep
Documentation
Documents
DoD Policy
Economics
Effectiveness
Effectiveness Eval
Elementary Sch Exp
Email
Emerg
Emp Dev
Emp Sfty and Welf
Employee
Employee Activities
Eng
Engineering Exp
Equip Maint/Monitor
Equipment Mgmt
Estimating
Evaluation
Evaluation Method
Experience
Facilities
Family Housing
Finance
Financial
Financial Status
Fiscal Mgmt
Follow Policy/Proc
Follow Rules/Regs
Forces

FORSCOM
Funding
Funds Allocation
Funds Analysis
Funds Mgmt/Control
General Supply
Goal Setting
Government Exp
Govt-Owned Property
Group Leadership
Health & Safety
HR
HR Communications
Identifies Problems
Identify
Information Tech/IS
Innovtn&Initiatve
Inspection
Interpersonal Skill
Intgratd Log
Inv Dist Mgmt
Item Mgmt
Job Description
Key Control
Language Arts
Law/Regs Interp
Leadership
Legal Documents
Liability
Liaising
Liaison
Library Exp
Logistics
Logistics Analysis
Logistics Data
Logistics Integratn
Logistics Issues
Logistics Mgmt Exp
Logistics Mgmt Sys
Logistics Operation
Logistics Plan
Logistics Principls
Logistics Support
Logistics System
Logstcs Emrg Tech

Maint/Repair Reqmt
Maintenance
Maintenance Support
Management
Management Systems
Management Training
Material Production
Material Storage
Materials
Meet Timeline
Member
Middle School Exp
Military Cmd
Military Experience
MIS
Mission Analysis
Monitor
Multi-Family
Obligate Funds
Occupational Health
Offcr
Operational
Oral
Organiz Change
Organiz Design
Performance
Performance Eval
Performing Acty
Personnel

Keywords in this announcement are highlighted. Find other keywords and circle them.

DEFENSE LOGISTICS AGENCY
The Warfighters Logistics Combat Support Agency

The Source Behind the Force

Department: Department Of Defense

Agency: Defense Logistics Agency

Job Announcement Number:
DLIS-09-2487

Program Analyst

SALARY RANGE: 46,625.00 - 73,329.00 USD /year

SERIES & GRADE: GS-0343-09/11

PROMOTION POTENTIAL: 11

OPEN PERIOD: Friday, May 22, 2009
to Wednesday, June 03, 2009

POSITION INFORMATION: Full Time Permanent

DUTY LOCATIONS: vacancy(s) in one of the following
locations: 1 vacancy - Battle Creek Metro area

MAJOR DUTIES:

Position Description # U3198 (GS-09)and U3197 (GS-11). Incumbent serves as a Program Analyst assisting senior analysts responsible for the life cycle management of Department of Defense Electronic Mall (DoD EMALL). Responsible for **system surveillance/monitoring, translating customer needs to system requirements, drafting requirements documents, managing change requests based on cost and schedule and executing test plans** to validate that changes will **meet customer needs**. Participates in the development, improvement and maintenance of the DoD EMALL and its processes. Incumbent assists senior analysts as advisor to customers of the DoD EMALL data systems, programs and processes. The DoD EMALL Branch is responsible for aiding in the accomplishment of the supply and logistics mission functions. **Develops effective, efficient and innovative information system solutions** to meet functional requirements. Participates in developing recommended policy and procedures, coordinates replies and findings made by agencies in the inspection of operational activities. Performs extensive coordination with logistics and systems experts in order to define issues and problems in areas where useful precedence does not exist. Serves as an advisor to senior analysts with regard to **achieving optimum effective utilization of standardized data processing systems and programs**. Recommends additional areas of utilization of automated equipment, systems and methods to facilitate **planning control, decision making and increased effectiveness of operation**. Works with technical representatives and staff members of DLA, the military services, civil agencies, foreign governments and Government contractors to assist senior analysts in providing oversight for DoD EMALL requirements definition, design, development, testing and implementation phases. Ensures system enhancements/system changes are collaborated with HQ DLA, military service representatives, and customers when required. Participates in the accomplishment of projects in the systems area that involve **problem analysis, developing draft solutions/ recommendations and improving the program as it relates to life cycle management of data systems**. Participates in **analyzing proposed benefits and costs of proposed system changes** and recommends action to management.

KEYWORDS FROM PROGRAM ANALYST POSITION

Add these keywords into your federal resume if applicable. Use some of these keywords as headings for the Outline Format resume (see samples in Step 6).

- System requirements
- System surveillance
- Monitoring, translating customer needs
- Test development
- Draft requirements documents manage change requirements
- Validate that changes meet customer needs
- Develop and maintain data systems
- Develop effective, efficient and innovative information solutions
- Achieve optimum utilization of standardized data processing systems
- Facilitate planning control for increased effectiveness of operation
- Problem analysis
- Develop draft solutions
- Life cycle management of data systems
- Analyze proposed benefits and costs of proposed system changes

> Try to find at least 10 keywords for each announcement that can go into your federal resume.

What are your keywords? Do they match the announcement (or almost)? Make a list here of keywords, including skills, proper names, programs, policies, and procedures that could become significant in your resume.

_____

_____

_____

_____

_____

_____

_____

_____

_____

_____

_____

_____

Introducing the Outline Format with keywords for your electronic federal resume.

Your federal resume is your job application, job examination, and sometimes the job interview.

This step-by-step chapter will help you gather the information, research the language you need to use, write the content, and format your resume correctly for multiple online resume builders, including USAJOBS.

You will learn how to:

1. Use the **Outline Format** for your electronic resume for the online builders to make the resume more readable and clearly list the keywords and skills from the announcement.

2. Develop the best match of your resume toward a target announcement to demonstrate your specialized experience and qualifications for the job.

3. Research the keywords, skills, and language for your future job to best focus your resume.

4. Sell yourself with your accomplishments and special projects to help you land the interview and the job.

5. Add your best core competencies to give value-added best impressions!

6. Include the most relevant and recent training and awards to help you to STAND OUT.

Federal resumes are different from private industry resumes for a number of reasons. Here is a quick list of differences to keep in mind when you are converting your private industry resume into a federal resume.

Private Industry and TAP Resume	Federal Resume
Typically 1-2 pages	3-5 pages based on specific character lengths (use full character lengths if possible)
Creative use of bold, underline, and other graphics are acceptable	Text file, chronological, traditional format with no graphics; use CAPS for enhancement in lieu of graphics.
No federal elements required (i.e., SSN, supervisor's name and phone, salary, veteran's preference, etc.)	Federal elements required (SSN, supervisor's name and phone, salary, veteran's preference, etc.)
Short accomplishment bullets focused on results	Accomplishment bullets focused on the details of "how" you attained results
Branded "headline"	Focus on the KSAs and competencies required in the announcement.
Keywords are important.	Keywords are imperative.
Focus on accomplishments; less details for position descriptions	Use blend of accomplishments and duties description with details.
Profit motivated, product oriented, select customer base	Fiscal responsibility and grants, budgets, cost control, implementation of programs, legislation, serving the American public

Additional Special Considerations for Military

Military	Federal Resume
List dates of Reserve service and active duty service.	Include approx. average hours for Reserve service, i.e., 20 years of Reserve service with deployments, equals six years of full-time work at 52 weeks per year.
Include applicable awards and indicate justification for attaining award.	List most awards and honors and include justification.
Translate military acronyms and jargon.	Translate most military acronyms and jargon, but use acronyms if the vacancy announcement uses the acronyms (i.e., DOD, DON, USMC, etc.).
Quantify and qualify military activities or acronyms.	Quantify and qualify military activities or acronyms.
Only include military schools/education related to the announcement.	Include military service schools; indicate resident classes and total hours.

What makes a resume "federal" are the following "compliance details" that must be included in your federal resume. Here is the information from the OPM webssite (www.usajobs.opm. gov/EI25.htm) regarding what to include in your resume.

Please include the following information in your resume:

Job Information

Announcement number, title, and grade.

Personal Information

Full name, mailing address (with ZIP code), day and evening phone numbers (with area code), Social Security number, country of citizenship, veterans' preference, reinstatement eligibility, and highest federal civilian grade held.

Education

Colleges or universities, name, city, and state, majors and type and year of any degrees received (if no degree, show total credits earned and indicate whether semester or quarter hours). High school name, city, and state. (Some announcements do not ask for high school.)

Work Experience

Job title, duties, and accomplishments, employer's name and address, supervisor's name and phone number, starting and ending dates (month and year), hours per week, salary, and indicate whether or not your current supervisor may be contacted. Prepare a separate entry for each job.

Other Qualifications

Job-related training courses (title and year), job-related skills, job-related certificates and licenses, job-related honors, awards, and special accomplishments.

DO

Collect Information

❑ Locate all of your written career papers, such as resumes, evaluations, and position descriptions.

❑ Find your list of training classes.

❑ Find or order you college transcripts.

❑ Find your DD-214 and other veteran's documents.

Research Announcements

❑ Find at least one announcement that is correct for you.

❑ Analyze the keywords from duties, qualifications, and questions.

❑ Analyze the one year specialized Experience that is important for your announcement.

Federal Resume Writing

❑ Make a list of accomplishments from your list two positions.

❑ Be sure to mention the types of customers you serve; and list the customers if you can.

❑ Write your first federal resume that will focus your resume toward one position.

❑ After you write ONE resume and target this toward ONE job series, you can write another resume version – with additional keywords.

❑ Count the characters for the builder, i.e., USAJOBS: 3,000 characters; DoD*ESS/ AVUE: 4,000 characters for each work experience.

❑ Proofread and edit the resume – have a second person read the resume if you can.

Formatting for Resume Builders with the Outline Format

❑ Use ALL CAPS selectively with small paragraphs for your builder resume.

❑ The ALL CAPS keywords should match the keywords in the announcement.

❑ Paragraphs in the BUILDER Federal resume should be 4 to 8 lines long.

Federal Resume Builders

❑ Copy and paste your resume into the various online builders.

❑ Preview the resume in the builder so you can correct any formatting problems.

DON'T

❑ Don't write one federal resume and use it for all of your positions.

❑ Don't just submit your TAP resume as your federal resume.

❑ Don't use too many acronyms.

❑ Don't copy and paste text straight from the announcement and your position description.

❑ Don't write your original resume in a builder (write the resume in software, then copy and paste into the builder).

❑ Don't write your federal resume in one paragraph (called the Big Block).

❑ Don't use a long list of bullets for your duties section.

The private industry or job fair resume is generally two pages long and is too short to be an effective federal resume.

Elizabeth Rogers
89 Mellor Avenue
Baltimore, MD 22128
Day Phone: 444-444-4444
Email: elizabeth@resume-place.com

Eligible: Noncompetitive Appointment of Certain Military Spouses, 5 CFR Parts 315 and 316
Veterans Preference: None
[or]
Veterans preference: 10-points derived preference

WORK EXPERIENCE	NAVAL STATION NAVSTA NAVSTA Financial Services Office Rota Spain	2/2009 - Present

Hours per week: 40

Administrative Assistant
• Team Lead for Administrative Staff (5 Americans and 2 Locals) for administrative and personnel functions for a military installation of over 1,500 personnel.
• Correspondence preparation, reporting functions and general administrative requirements for financial, payroll and tenant services on the base.
• Maintained time and attendance reports for civilian staff.
• Handled pay and leave requests from both civilian and military personnel.
• Maintained knowledge of military pay and leave regulations as stated in the DoD Directive 1327.5 and OPNAV 1050.3.
• Handling appointment schedules, plans, personal correspondence, and documents for complex international and domestic travel.
• Managed daily tasks. Ensured accurate completion of all tasks in a timely manner.
• Edited Standard Operating Procedures such as mobilization and ration control. Wrote formal letters and memos on behalf of the company commander.
• Supervised and managed the unit's library of publications and filing systems in accordance with Army regulations.

Don't forget to format your federal resume, even in the resume builder. Typing a large block of text is very difficult for the human resources person to scan or read.

Elizabeth Rogers
89 Mellor Avenue
Baltimore, MD 22128
Day Phone: 444-444-4444
Email: elizabeth@resume-place.com

WORK EXPERIENCE NAVAL STATION NAVSTA   **2/2009 - Present**
NAVSTA Financial Services
Office Rota Spain

Hours per week: 40

Administrative Assistant

TEAM LEAD FOR ADMINISTRATIVE STAFF (5 Americans and 2 Locals) for administrative and personnel functions for a military installation of over 1,500 personnel. Provided technical advice on correspondence preparation, reporting functions and general administrative requirements for financial, payroll and tenant services on the base. Reported to the Senior NCO for Administration. MAINTAINED HUMAN RESOURCES DOCUMENTS including of performance management, training, certifications,, quarterly counseling and annual evaluations for senior officers. Maintained time and attendance reports for civilian staff. HANDLED PAY AND LEAVE REQUESTS from both civilian and military personnel. Maintained knowledge of military pay and leave regulations as stated in the DoD Directive 1327.5 and OPNAV 1050.3. Coordinated higher headquarters and subordinate units to include all personnel actions, Uniform Code of Military Justice (UCMJ) actions, and travel requests. ADMINISTRATIVE ASSISTANT TO THE DIRECTOR handling appointment schedules, plans, personal correspondence and documents. Complex international and domestic travel. PLANNED, PRIORITIZED AND ORGANIZED DAILY TASKS IN MULTIPLE AREAS. Ensured accurate completion of all tasks in a timely manner. EDITED STANDARD OPERATING PROCEDURES FOR COMPANY POLICY such as mobilization and ration control. Wrote formal letters and memos on behalf of the company commander. Supervised and managed the unit's library of publications and filing systems in accordance with Army regulations. Revamped and updated the unit's previously outdated filing system and library of regulations, bringing it in accordance with Navy regulations. This contributed to a 100 percent rating in a later Inspector General's (IG) inspection. Facilitated and resolved back log of requests for transportation needs related to a soldiers returning home after several-month stop loss.

FAMILY MEMBER -- USAJOBS RESUME IN OUTLINE FORMAT

This outline format is the best resume to use for the federal resume builder, It is readable, impressive, and targeted for the vacancy announcement. It also includes keywords from the announcement and accomplishments.
Target: Secretary (OA), GS-0318-6, GS-8

Elizabeth Rogers
89 Mellor Avenue
Baltimore, MD 22128
Day Phone: 444-444-4444
Email: elizabeth@resume-place.com

Country of citizenship:	United States of America
Veterans' Preference:	10 Points Derived Preference, 5 CFR 315.612
Contact Current Employer:	No

WORK EXPERIENCE	**NAVAL STATION** **NAVSTA Financial Services** **Office, Rota, Spain**	**2/2006 - 12/2008** **Grade Level: GS-5** **Hours per week: 40**

ADMINISTRATIVE ASSISTANT, 318

TEAM LEAD FOR ADMINISTRATIVE STAFF (5 Americans and 2 Locals) for administrative and personnel functions for a military installation of over 1,500 personnel. Provided **technical advice on correspondence preparation, reporting functions and general administrative requirements for** financial, payroll, and tenant services on the base. Reported to the Senior NCO for Administration.

MAINTAINED HUMAN RESOURCES DOCUMENTS including of performance management, training, certifications, quarterly counseling and annual evaluations for senior officers. Maintained **time and attendance reports** for civilian staff.

HANDLED PAY AND LEAVE REQUESTS from both civilian and military personnel. Maintained knowledge of military pay and leave regulations as stated in the DoD Directive 1327.5 and OPNAV 1050.3. Coordinated higher headquarters and subordinate units to include all personnel actions, Uniform Code of Military Justice (UCMJ) actions, and **travel requests.**

ADMINISTRATIVE ASSISTANT TO THE DIRECTOR handling appointment schedules, plans, personal **correspondence,** and documents. Complex international and domestic travel.

PLANNED, PRIORITIZED, AND ORGANIZED DAILY TASKS IN MULTIPLE AREAS. Ensured accurate completion of all tasks in a timely manner.

EDITED STANDARD OPERATING PROCEDURES FOR COMPANY POLICY such as mobilization and ration control. **Wrote formal letters and memos** on behalf of the company commander. Supervised and managed the unit's **library of publications and filing systems** in accordance with Army regulations.

KEY ACCOMPLISHMENTS:
+ Revamped and updated the unit's previously outdated filing system and library of regulations, bringing it in accordance with **Navy regulations.** This contributed to a 100 percent rating in a later Inspector General's (IG) inspection.
+ Facilitated and resolved back log of 200 requests for transportation needs related to soldiers returning home after several-month stop loss.

UNITED STATES NAVY   1/2005 - 2/2006
Postal and Technical Order
Distribution Center Operations
PATUXENT NAVAL AIR STATION
MD US

Grade Level: GS-4

Hours per week: 40

ADMINISTRATIVE SPECIALIST/MAIL CLERK , 318
PREPARED AND PROCESSED ALL PERSONNEL ACTIONS to include Uniform Code of Military Justice (UCMJ) actions and **travel requests. Extracted and analyzed data** from various sources to prepare **reports** and complete projects. Developed, implemented, and maintained **filing systems** and **libraries of regulations.**

DRAFTED MEMOS AND LETTERS for the commanding officer related to company **policies and procedures;** disseminated **correspondence** to higher headquarters regarding personnel recommendations for promotions and awards. Wrote minutes for company leaders' monthly board meeting. Accurately typed **correspondence** (formal letters, memos, statistical reports) to higher headquarters and subordinate units.

MANAGED AND DISTRIBUTED MAIL, processed all certified and registered mail, and maintained records in accordance with the United States Postal Service. **Complied with all privacy laws, rules, and regulations.**

ERA Real Estate
CORONADO, CA US

6/2002 - 12/2004

Salary: 25000 USD Per Year
Hours per week: 50

REALTY OFFICE ASSISTANT

EXCELLENT CUSTOMER SERVICE for homebuyers and sellers. Developed lists and qualified sales prospects for 10 agents. Scheduled advertising and property inspections. Prepared contracts for realtors and closing attorneys.

INTERPERSONAL SKILLS: Supported working relationships and schedules with other realtors, attorneys, title agents, inspectors, builders, trades workers, financial agents, city and state agencies. Honored all confidentiality issues.

KNOWLEDGE OF REAL ESTATE LAWS, GUIDELINES, AND REGULATIONS. Maintained thorough and accurate records to meet state and federal guidelines.

TRAINING:
+ Completed ERA Sales Training Course

EDUCATION

UNIVERSITY OF MARYLAND, UNIVERSITY COLLEGE
Distance Learning, current
Seeking B.S. in Business Administration; 34 credits completed in total
2006 courses: Business Administration (3 hrs), Human Resources Management (3)
2007 courses: Intro to Economics (3 hrs), Statistics (3 hrs)

CORONADO COMMUNITY COLLEGE
Coronado, CA, US
Some College Coursework Completed
18 Semester Hours
Major: BUSINESS ADMINISTRATION
Relevant Coursework, Licensures and Certifications:
6 semester hours of accounting and finance coursework.

CATONSVILLE HIGH SCHOOL, CATONSVILLE, MD, 1999

TRAINING

ANNE ARUNDEL COMMUNITY COLLEGE, MD US, 1/2005 to 1/2006
Continuing Education Classes:
Introduction to Keyboarding, Working with Windows, Managing Your Files and Folders (My Documents), Quickbooks for Small Business Accounting

ADDITIONAL INFORMATION

ELIGIBLE: NONCOMPETITIVE SPOUSE SEEKING FEDERAL POSITION
ADMINISTRATIVE ASSISTANT AND PROGRAM ANALYST

Seeking a federal position utilizing my Noncompetitive Spouse Appointment of Certain Military Spouses. I have relocated (PCS) with my family to _____ and would like to begin my federal career here in a GS 7-9 position.

Summary of Qualifications:
5 years Administrative experience
Solid Microsoft Office skills, including expert Excel
Proven abilities in scheduling, coordination and planning
Expert in analyzing efficiency and effectiveness of program offices
Flexible, willing, highly-competent, friendly and professional
Quick learner at new programs, systems and customer requirements
Team player with solid communications skills

NONCOMPETITIVE APPOINTMENT DOCUMENTATION ATTACHED:
DD-214 of spouse
Marriage Certificate
PCS orders

COMPUTER SKILLS:
+ Type 50+ WPM.
+ Word and Basic Excel – create and update spreadsheets
+ Outlook and email management services
+ Power Point - development and updates
+ Internet (Explorer) – research skills

VOLUNTEER ACTIVITIES:

Rota, Spain, 5 hours per week, 1/2007 to 7/2008
ENGLISH INSTRUCTOR: In off-duty time, taught an English class to approximately 25 local employees assigned to the base to improve their verbal and written proficiency.

Patuxent River NAS, MD – 2/2005-2006, 10 hours per week
FAMILY AND MORALE, RECREATION AND WELFARE VOLUNTEER. Event planning team member, coordinator for volunteers and marketing assistant. Updated the mailing lists for program participants and marketing with fliers throughout the base. Events planned and coordinated included: deep sea fishing, runner's events, Right Arm Night.

Coronado NAS, Coronado, CA , 1/2003-12/2004; 10 hours per week
OMBUDSMAN AND SOLDIER TO FAMILY ADVOCATE, WARRIOR IN TRANSITION PROGRAM. In this new program, I advocated for family members and returning soldiers needing special health care, physical disability processing and medical services. I maintained records and gave referrals to transition services to the Veteran's Administration.

The private industry or job fair resume is generally two pages long and is too short to be an effective federal resume.

Timothy W. Tarka

2503 Clements Bridge Rd.
Jacksonville Beach, FL 32250
Home: 815-777-0000

EMPLOYMENT HISTORY

05/2007-present, 40+ hours per week, SUPPLY QUALITY ASSURANCE FIRST LINE SUPERVISOR, USS CARL VINSON (CVN-70), Bremerton, WA 98312. CDR Jeff Johnson, 333-555-4444. Permission to contact.

During 2-year assignment to USS Carl Vinson, completely revitalized Quality Assurance Program.

- Managed and prepared for major supply management inspection.
- Supervised quality assurance auditors and analyzed supply divisions.
- Directed and trained 71 supply personnel.
- Trained in customer services supply policies and procedures.
- Interpreted and implemented policies and directives for requisition processing; weapon system and acquisition management.
- To improve inventory management, conducted supply operations audits to determine application of improved methods.
- Collected, reviewed and collated supply metric reports.
- Tracked and maintained complex spreadsheets.
- Developed, presented and critiqued firefighting training and informational sessions.
- Trained and qualified 55 personnel in firefighting procedures.
- Performed full range of firefighting tasks.
- Operated fire extinguishing agents, including 45-pound CO_2, PKP and AFFF.

Don't forget to format your federal resume, even in the resume builder. Typing a large block of text is very difficult for the human resources person to scan or read.

Timothy W. Tarka

2503 Clements Bridge Rd.
Jacksonville Beach, FL 32250
Home: 815-777-0000

EMPLOYMENT HISTORY

05/2007-present, 40+ hours per week, SUPPLY QUALITY ASSURANCE FIRST LINE SUPERVISOR, USS CARL VINSON (CVN-70), Bremerton, WA 98312. CDR Jeff Johnson, 333-555-4444. Permission to contact.

During 2-year assignment to USS Carl Vinson, completely revitalized Quality Assurance Program. ANALYZED AND ADMINISTERED SUPPLY OPERATIONS to meet changing customer requirements: Hand-picked to fill Lead Chief role in Quality Assurance Division and direct day-to-day operations during 9.5 month Western Pacific deployment. Demonstrated expertise in analyzing the systems for procurement, automatic data processing, warehouse management, distribution and quality assurance. Managed and prepared for major supply management inspection. Supervised 6 quality assurance auditors and analyzed 14 supply divisions and their working relationship with supply and maintenance management tools, i.e., Relational Supply (RSUPPLY), Integrated Barcode System (IBS) and Naval Aviation Logistics Command Information Systems (NALCOMIS). Gave presentations and briefings on the new supply systems. Directed and trained 71 supply personnel. Trained in customer services supply policies and procedures. Interpreted and implemented policies and directives for requisition processing; weapon system and acquisition management; weapon systems life-cycle management; project management; and budget estimate and execution. Reviewed and improved marketing of supply services to customers. To improve inventory management, conducted supply operations audits to determine application of improved methods. Collected, reviewed and collated supply metric reports from 14 managers. Tracked and maintained complex spreadsheets for financial reports, inventory and location audit process. Developed, presented and critiqued firefighting training and informational sessions. Trained and qualified 55 personnel in firefighting procedures. Planned, managed and critiqued 95 ship-wide firefighting drills.Served as Damage Control Training Team member; responded to alarms and major emergencies. Performed full range of firefighting tasks, including combating fires involving structures, equipment, facilities, as well as fuel and chemical fires, controlling and extinguishing fires while performing rescues. Operated fire extinguishing agents, including 45-pound CO_2, PKP and AFFF.

MILITARY SERVICE MEMBER, E-6, US Navy

Federal Resume In Word – Ready To Copy And Paste Into A Resume Builder
Target: Supply Specialist, GS-9/11

Timothy W. Tarka
2503 Clements Bridge Rd.
Jacksonville Beach, FL 32250
Home: 815-777-0000
TWTarka1@aol.com
SSN: 111-22-3333
Veterans Preference: 5 points
Citizenship: U.S.

EMPLOYMENT HISTORY

05/2007-present, 40+ hours per week, SUPPLY QUALITY ASSURANCE FIRST LINE SUPERVISOR, USS CARL VINSON (CVN-70), Bremerton, WA 98312. CDR Jeff Johnson, 333-555-4444. Permission to contact.

During 2-year assignment to USS Carl Vinson, completely revitalized Quality Assurance Program.

ANALYZED AND ADMINISTERED SUPPLY OPERATIONS to meet changing customer requirements; hand-picked to fill Lead Chief role in Quality Assurance Division and direct day-to-day operations during 9.5 month Western Pacific deployment. Demonstrated expertise in analyzing the systems for procurement, automatic data processing, warehouse management, distribution, and quality assurance. Managed and prepared for major supply management inspection. Supervised 6 quality assurance auditors and analyzed 14 supply divisions and their working relationship with supply and maintenance management tools, i.e., Relational Supply (RSUPPLY), Integrated Barcode System (IBS) and Naval Aviation Logistics Command Information Systems (NALCOMIS). Gave PRESENTATIONS and briefings on the new supply systems.

IMPROVED CUSTOMER SERVICES AND SUPPLY SYSTEM MANAGEMENT: Directed and trained 71 supply personnel. Trained in customer services supply policies and procedures. Interpreted and implemented policies and directives for requisition processing; weapon system and acquisition management; weapon systems life-cycle management; project management; and budget estimate and execution. Reviewed and improved marketing of supply services to customers.

RESEARCHED AND ANALYZED SUPPLY ITEM SPECIFICATIONS: To improve inventory management, conducted supply operations audits to determine application of improved methods. Collected, reviewed, and collated supply metric reports from 14 managers. Tracked and maintained complex spreadsheets for financial reports, inventory, and location audit process.

KEY ACCOMPLISHMENTS:

+ Developed first supply management inspection checklist for all 17 functional areas of supply. Included 570 spot checks, ensuring all areas of supply procedures, policy, and methods were audited monthly. Checklist was issued as a handbook, to assure that SOPs were daily practice, and served as model for all 6 Pacific Fleet Aircraft Carriers.
+ Planned and coordinated 22 underway replenishments in support of Operation Iraqi Freedom. Determined distribution and positioning of 7,447 pallets. Loaded, unloaded, and delivered supplies among 41 using actives.

03/2005-05/2007, 40+ hours per week, AVIATION SUPPORT DIVISION LEADING PETTY OFFICER, USS CARL VINSON CVN-70, Bremerton, WA 98312. CDR Jeff Johnson, 333-555-4444. Permission to contact.

Directed day-to-day aviation supply operations while deployed to the Western Pacific and Arabian Gulf and supporting 75 tactical aircraft during Operation Enduring Freedom. Supervised diverse staff of 83 supply technicians; led 4 supply support sections and 11 storerooms.

INVENTORY MANAGEMENT: Administered warehouse-managing systems, entering physical counts through IBS. Oversaw stock maintenance at prescribed levels for 7,346 line items worth $450 million. Selected and structured 3 10-person inventory and inspection teams. Maintained records and control over material in stock and due-in; planned distribution system on quantitative and monetary basis.

Searched Federal Logistics (FEDLOG). Utilized military standard requisitioning procedures to process and issue 61,386 documents and processed 28,248 receipt documents worth $163 million in aviation repairables.

INVENTORY DISCREPANCIES: Conducted daily inventory analysis by reconciling 4,400 line items worth $250 million. Performed monthly reconciliation on NALCOMIS reports; analyzed mismatch and corrected errors. Reconciled inventory discrepancies from $1.8 million to $71,000. Achieved 100 percent inventory rate and "outstanding" grade during 11/2002 Supply Management Inspection.

ANALYSIS: Recommended system and program changes to improve timelines. Reviewed and analyzed operational reports, plans, work schedule, and planned requirements; determined and advised on compatibility of planned support program. Conducted special supply and demand studies, advised on procedures to be followed, reviewed financial data to determine reprogramming requirements. Maintained, adjusted, and established requisitions objectives, retention levels, maintenance, and proper disposition of serviceable and unserviceable assets. Used variety of auditing, reconciliation, and Military Standard Requisitioning and Issue Procedures (MILSTRIP).

PRODUCT MOVEMENT: Controlled distribution and redistribution of stock. Orchestrated transfer and delivery of 246 excess line items worth $18 million to deployed Navy ships. Reduced re-distributable assets on board within agency goal of 3%.

KEY ACCOMPLISHMENTS:
+ Led division in arduous wartime OPTEMPO during Operation Enduring Freedom, 111 straight days at sea. Tracked 18,700 Depot level repairables through the repair cycle. Achieved highest accountability levels seen at the Type Commander. Led Vertical Onboard Delivery (VOD) teams in transferring over 3,000 pallets with no loss.
+ Ensured Rotatable Pool (R-POOL), Local Repair Cycle Assets (LRCA) stock and proved team was ready for deployment 9 months ahead of schedule. Achieved 100% range, 99% depth, and accommodation factor of 65%, all well above Type Commander goals.

02/2003-03/2005. 40+ hours per week, LOGISTICS AND MATERIAL CONTROL FIRST LINE SUPERVISOR. Helicopter Combat Support Squadron-FIVE (HC-5), Yigo, Guam 96915. SKC Frank Maceo, 677-989-9898.

Provided logistics support and material control in support of the U.S. Seventh Fleet and U.S. Naval Forces Central Command. Managed 47 personnel in support of 13 CH-46 aircraft and 6 organizations deployed throughout Asia.

SUPPLY SYSTEMS MANAGEMENT: Integrated logistical requirements into comprehensive plan for management techniques, supply procedures, automated data processing equipment, and control. Conducted analytical studies for quantitative and budgetary forecast, procurement authorization, funds management, and distribution or redistribution of materiel. Managed logistical plan from initial planning to acquisition, storage, issue, and disposal. Managed 16,000 line items valued at $26 million.

REQUIREMENTS ANALYSIS: Tracked critical aviation requirements and developed long and short-range material plans. Used Fleet Inventory Management and Reporting System (FIMARS) to determine Total Asset Visibility (TAV) for deployed detachments. Prepared, delivered, and issued material to shops and work centers. Kept local stock records and reordered low stock as appropriate. Prepared material and procurement directives and made recommendations and authorizations.

FUNDS MANAGEMENT: Determined funds, quantities and categories. Scheduled, analyzed, and forecast material requirement. Managed $900,000 budget.

MATERIAL DISTRIBUTION / MANAGEMENT: Planned distribution and positioned supplies among major supply stations, stock points, and using activities. Researched, coordinated, procured, validated, received, and distributed nearly 71,300 requisitions for parts. Maintained ready-for-use tools and controlled issuance of calibration equipment. Maintained 100% accountability of Individual Material Readiness List (IMRL) items.

SENIOR SECTION LEADER: Managed oversight of 250 personnel in 4 duty rosters. Responded to physical security needs, typhoon preparations, and 24-hour search and rescue operations for Guam and the Northern Marianas.

02/1999-02/2003, 40+ hours per week, INSTRUCTOR TRAINER. Fleet Aviation Specialized Operational Training Group Atlantic (FASOTRAGRULANT). Jacksonville, FL 32212. AZC Jose Cravioto.

INSTRUCTOR: Assigned to Aviation Maintenance Administration and Management Training (AMAMT) Division, instructing aviation supply courses for 200 students annually.

CURRICULUM DEVELOPMENT: Directed and reviewed implementation of Chief of Naval Operation instruction (OPNAVINST 4790.2F). Rewrote over 20 courses of instruction and respective classroom support materials.

TRAINER DEVELOPMENT: Trained, evaluated, and mentored newly assigned instructors in technical skill sets, supply policy and procedures.

EDUCATION

James A. Shanks, FL 32351, Diploma, 1995
English Composition 1, University of Maryland, Santa Rita, GUAM. 2001
English 301 and 310, American Preparatory Institution, Killeen, TX. 2000

PROFESSIONAL TRAINING

Evaluations Fitness Report, Chief of Naval Education Training, 8 hours, 01/2009
Command Training Team Indoctrination Course, Naval Station Guam, 21 hours, 05/2008
Leadership and Management Training, Afloat Training Group Pacific, 21 hours, 03/2005
Naval Aviation Visual Information Display System and Maintenance Action Form and SCIR
Documentation, Fleet Aviation Specialized Operational Training Group Atlantic, 40 hours, 02/1996
(Full training list upon request.)

AWARDS, HONORS, AND RECOGNITIONS

Distinguished Service Award
Navy and Marine Corps Achievement Medals (2)
Good Conduct Medals (6)
National Defense Service Medal (6)
Navy Unit Commendation (2)
Navy "E" Ribbon (3)

OTHER INFORMATION

SUMMARY: In-depth, demonstrated knowledge of supply operations, methods, and systems with 22
years of experience. Proven ability to manage and direct critical supply programs, including property
management, accounting and acquisition, equipment reutilization and repair, and all logistics. Skilled in
improving inventory tracking and record-keeping and resolving discrepancies. Known ability to analyze
supply readiness and monitor trends in supply system performance. Specialized experience in
management of aviation supply, medicine, food, and other perishables.

Accomplished leader, able to take charge and direct staff in stressful situations while maintaining
composure. Effective communicator, skilled in working effectively with individuals of all organizational
levels in courteous, tactful manner. Ability to analyze, learn, and implement complex rules and regulations
and make prompt decisions.

COMPUTER PROFICIENCIES: MS Office: Outlook, PowerPoint, Word, Excel; Windows

❑ Provide ALL the information requested including documentation required for the position.

❑ Answer ALL job-related questions to the best of your ability. Include accurate details of your experience, education, or training in the narrative input fields provided.

❑ Use ALL portions of the application to provide unique and exemplary information that sets you apart from other candidates.

❑ Present your most important job-related competencies and accomplishments.

❑ Read the vacancy announcement carefully from top to bottom.

❑ Stress actions and achievements.

❑ Present information in a polished (and accurate!) manner.

❑ Count your characters in your job blocks:
- USAJOBS has 3,000 character limit per job.
- AvueCentral has 4,000 character limit per job.
- Army CPOL has 12,000 characters for ALL JOBS.
- DONHR has 7,000 characters per job.

SELL YOURSELF!

FEDERAL RESUME WRITING FACTS AND TIPS

- ❑ Use ALL CAPS for official position titles, titles of roles in jobs, or unofficial, working job titles, such as PROJECT MANAGER, SENIOR STAFF ADVISOR, RECEPTIONIST. All caps can be used to identify major functional areas of work. Do not overuse.
- ❑ Keep your paragraph length to eight to ten lines.
- ❑ Use more nouns. Nouns are searchable terms in most databases. For example, use "editor" rather than "responsible for compiling documents and preparing a publication."

- ❑ Use plain language. Write professionally and concisely.
- ❑ Eliminate acronyms whenever possible. When you must use them, spell them out once.
- ❑ Space is limited, so drop words that do not add value.
- ❑ Avoid using the same descriptor twice in the same paragraph.
- ❑ Start each sentence with an action verb, and not "I." Use the personal pronoun "I" two times per page, to remind the reader that it is YOUR resume.
- ❑ Active voice is more powerful than passive voice.
- ❑ Use present tense for present work experience, past tense for previous work experience or for projects in the present work experience that have ended. Write in the first person, without the use of "I" and do not add "s" to your verbs, i.e. plans or manages.
- ❑ Include the proper names and generic descriptions of products, software, and equipment.
- ❑ Federal resumes must include compliance details for each job for the last ten years.
- ❑ Prior to ten years: if the positions are relevant, include the title of your job, organization, city, state, and dates. A short one-sentence description can be included.
- ❑ Begin with your most recent position and work backward, unless you need to highlight a position that is relevant and not the most recent.
- ❑ Military assignments: list the most recent ones first. Include many details on the last ten years. Anything longer than ten years, summarize and edit the text to include only the relevant experience.
- ❑ Retired Military: combine early positions/assignments.
- ❑ Students: include relevant positions only.
- ❑ Unpaid volunteer experience is equal to paid work experience for federal job qualifications. If you are using unpaid work to qualify, summarize your volunteer experience under Community Service and include the number of hours per week in your description.
- ❑ Missing years of experience? Just skip those years and write great descriptions about the positions you have held. However, be prepared to discuss it in an interview.
- ❑ Returning to government after leaving? Feature your GOVERNMENT EXPERIENCE first, then list your BUSINESS OR OTHER EXPERIENCE second.

Have you heard that KSAs may be eliminated?

The traditional essays for the knowledge, skills, and abilities (KSAs) statements could soon be eliminated. President Obama signed a memorandum to make immediate hiring reforms on May 11, 2010. See details at www.opm.gov/hiringreform/.

What does this mean for you?

Though you may no longer need to write long, cumbersome essays as part of your federal job application, you STILL need to somehow demonstrate that you do in fact have the knowledge, skills, and abilities to perform the job duties described in the vacancy announcement. How to do this will depend on the application.

Then how will you demonstrate your KSAs?

Currently, there are two main ways to demonstrate your KSAs:

1. Assessment Questionnaires with Short Examples and Essays Demonstrating Your Accomplishment Record

These are becoming more and more popular. You might see them called "applicant questionnaires," "occupational questionnaires," or "assessment questionnaire" in Application Manager. These are usually a list of multiple choice type questions, and you may be asked to explain an answer with a short essay.

2. KSAs / Accomplishment Record in the Federal Resume

An accomplishment record, like a traditional KSA essay, is in fact a longer written essay with paragraphs but are more specific than KSAs. Write about one or two major accomplishments that relate to the job duties described. These accomplishments do not have to be work related. They can be from volunteer work, community service, training, or school.

The Outline Format can include your KSAs easily with the ALL CAP HEADINGS. You can feature COMMUNICATIONS, WRITING, PROJECT MANAGEMENT, PLANNING AND COORDINATING and other KSAs or significant competencies as headings. The text under the headings can be examples from your Accomplishment Record that will demonstrate your KSAs.

Definition

Knowledge:

An organized body of information, usually of a factual or procedural nature, which, if applied, makes adequate performance on the job possible.

Skills:

The proficient manual, verbal, or mental manipulation of data, people, or things. Observable, quantifiable, measureable.

Abilities:

The power to perform an activity at the present time. Implied is a lack of discernible barriers, either physical or mental, to performing the activity.

Write your KSA answers by giving examples that demonstrate that particular knowledge, skill, or ability.

KSAs are also known as:

- Selective Placement Factors
- Narrative Statements
- Essays
- Examples
- Quality Ranking Factors
- Key Elements
- Specialized Qualifications
- Technical & Managerial Qualifications

How KSAs Were Rated and Ranked

The KSAs are "graded" by federal personnelists against a "crediting plan." The descriptions you write in your KSAs can result in a low or high grade. The total number of points adjusted for veterans' preference, if applicable, will determine if you are Best Qualified and if your application will be forwarded to the selecting official or panel for an interview.

The Crediting Plan is not available to job applicants. You just have to write the most impressive examples you can in your KSAs by giving the full context, the challenge of the project, your actions, and the results.

★ TEN RULES FOR WRITING KSAS OR ACCOMPLISMENTS

1 One excellent example per narrative will demonstrate that you have the knowledge, skills, and abilities for the position.

2 If possible and appropriate, use a different example in each accomplishment statement.

3 The typical length is ½ page per answer.

WOW!

Write your accomplishment examples with specific details, including the challenge of the example and the results. 4

Spell out ALL acronyms. 5

6 Write in the first person. "I serve as a point-of-contact for all inquiries that come to our office."

7 Quantify your results and accomplishments.

8 Draw material from all parts of your life, including community service, volunteer projects, or training.

9 Limit your paragraphs to 6 to 8 lines long for readability.

10

Proofread your writing again and again.

Example #1: KSAs on Separate Sheets of Paper -- Rated and Ranked by HR

Prepare written justification to the following KSAs as an attachment to your resume/ application.

Job Title: Lead Medical Supply Technician
Department: Department Of Veterans Affairs
Agency: Veterans Affairs, Veterans Health Administration

SALARY RANGE:	38,790.00 - 50,431.00 USD /year
SERIES & GRADE:	GS-0622-7/7
DUTY LOCATIONS:	1 vacancy - Lexington, KY

HOW YOU WILL BE EVALUATED:

All applicants should provide clear, concise examples that show the levels of accomplishment or degree to which they possess the KSAO's. Incomplete, vague, or contradictory information may affect the rating. Responses may be made on VA Form 5-4676a, Employee Supplemental Qualification Statement or a written supplemental on plain paper in a narrative format which addresses each item below separately. Candidates will be interviewed utilizing the Performance Based Interview (PBI) process. Questions will be job-related, reasonably consistent, and fair to all candidates. To learn more about PBI, you can visit the following two web sites: (1)   (2)
                    . Additionally, printed reference material is available at each Human Resources Office.

1. Ability to supervise staff of medical supply technicians. (Describe your experience in assigning and reviewing work, and explaining work requirements and providing training.)

2. Knowledge of variety of medical supply items/equipment used in a central supply area or operating room.

3. Knowledge of decontamination and sterilization.

4. Ability to manage multiple priorities and respond to demands.

5. Ability to communicate orally.

EXAMPLE #2: KSAs in the Resume

As part of the online process, you will need to respond to a series of questions designed to assess your passion of the following knowledges, skills and abilities. These KSAs should be included within the text of your resume, not on separate sheets of paper.

Job Title: **ADMINISTRATIVE OFFICER, GS-0341-9/11**

Department: **Department Of The Interior**
Agency: **Bureau of Indian Affairs**
Job Announcement Number: **AB-10-62**

SALARY RANGE:	47,448.00 - 74,628.00 USD /year
OPEN PERIOD:	Wednesday, April 14, 2010 to Wednesday, May 05, 2010
SERIES & GRADE:	GS-0341-09/11
POSITION INFORMATION:	Full TimeCareer/Career Conditional
PROMOTION POTENTIAL:	11
DUTY LOCATIONS:	1 vacancy - Fort Thompson, SD
WHO MAY BE CONSIDERED:	BUREAU-WIDE / INDIAN PREFERENCE ELIGIBLES / CURRENT STATUS EMPLOYEES OR FORMER EMPLOYEES WITH REINSTATEMENT ELIGIBILITY

HOW YOU WILL BE EVALUATED:

Do not overstate or understate your level of experience and demonstrated capability. You should be aware that your ratings are subject to evaluation and verification based on the résumé, and other relevant documents you submit, as well as through verification of references as appropriate. Later steps in the selection process are specifically designed to verify your stated level of experience and demonstrated capability. Deliberate attempts to falsify information may be grounds for not selecting you or for dismissing you from the position following acceptance.

As part of the online process, you will need to respond to a series of questions designed to assess your possession of the following knowledges, skills, and abilities:

- KNOWLEDGE OF FEDERAL ADMINISTRATIVE POLICIES REGARDING BUDGET AND FINANCE; PERSONNEL MANAGEMENT; PROCUREMENT; FORMS AND RECORDS MANAGEMENT.
- KNOWLEDGE OF ACCOUNTING AND BOOKKEEPING PROCEDURES; AND OF THE BUREAU ACCOUNTING SYSTEM AND PROCEDURES.
- KNOWLEDGE OF PUBLIC LAW 93-638, AS AMENDED, CONTRACTING AND GRANT REGULATIONS, GUIDELINES AND PROCEDURES.

EXAMPLE #3: KSAs in the Asssessment Questionnaire

Sometimes KSA narratives are requested in the assessment questionnaire. You may want to check the assessment questionnaire for the announcement first to see whether narratives are required. This particular announcement had 49 questions and 27 total narratives! You will want to know that in advance to plan the amount of time it will take you to complete the application.

The Office of Personnel Management has a recommended format for writing KSAs and your accomplishments record in a story-telling format.

Introducing the Context, Challenge, Action, Results (CCAR) Model for writing better KSAs:

CONTEXT

The context should include the role you played in this example. Were you a team member, planner, organizer, facilitator, administrator, or coordinator? Also, include your job title at the time and the timeline of the project. You may want to note the name of the project or situation.

CHALLENGE

What was the specific problem that you faced that needed resolution? Describe the challenge of the situation. The problem could be disorganization in the office, new programs that needed to be implemented or supported, a change in management, a major project stalled, or a large conference or meeting being planned. The challenge can be difficult to write about. You can write the challenge last when you are drafting your KSAs.

ACTION

What did you do that made a difference? Did you change the way the office processed information, responded to customers, managed programs? What did you do?

RESULT

What difference did it make? Did this new action save dollars or time? Did it increase accountability and information? Did the team achieve its goals?

This CCAR story-telling format is also great for the Behavior-Based Interview. Write your accomplishment "stories" and prepare for the Interview Examination. The VA announcement on page 85 states that the Behavior-based or Performance Based Interview will be part of the hiring process:

"Candidates will be interviewed utilizing the Performance Based Interview (PBI) process. Questions will be job-related, reasonably consistent, and fair to all candidates. To learn more about PBI, you can visit the following two web sites: (1) http://www. va.gov/pbi (2) http://vaww.va.gov/ohrm/Staffing/PBI/PBI_intr.htm."

Please write a work or non-work related example to support a particular KSA or example required in an Assessment Questionnaire. Write your CCAR stories and accomplishments for the questionnaire examples, the behavior-based interview, and a short version for your federal resume.

CONTEXT:

CHALLENGE:

ACTIONS:

1.

2.

3.

4.

RESULTS:

RECOGNITION/AWARD:

THREE KINDS OF KSAS AND ACCOMPLISHMENTS
Short KSAs / Essays and Examples of Accomplishments in the CCAR format
Longer KSA Narratives in CCAR for executives or complex examples
KSAs in the resume in the Outline Format

KSA SAMPLE 1 - Short KSA/Essays/Example

When KSAs are written on separate sheets of paper, the typical length is a 1/2 page for each. One or two examples can be written that will demonstrate your experience in this Knowledge, Skill, or Ability. Here is an example which follow the CCAR story-telling formula.

FAMILY MEMBER
Target: Secretary (OA), GS-0318-6

---

1. Knowledge of laws, rules, and regulations and ability to apply appropriate procedures in connection with payments, collections, or entitlements

Context: In my Administrative Assistant position in the Finance Office, Rota, Spain for 14 months, I HANDLED PAY REQUESTS and problem-solving from both civilian and military personnel. Maintained knowledge of military pay and leave regulations as stated in the Code of Military Personnel Regulations.

Challenge: I was a point of contact for soldiers returning from specialized training and deployments throughout CONUS and OCONUS.

Actions: I researched and resolved complex pay issues for soldiers and officers in support of deployment activities, travel, and repayment of expenses. I investigated databases for payment information, and followed up to ensure they were paid.

Results: Communicated with Defense Finance and Accounting Office Vendor representatives in Indianapolis to research problems and ensure payment. Was successful at establishing a contact who was responsive to my inquiries within 24 to 48 hours for numerous problem payment requests.

---

2. Ability to reach sound and justifiable decisions and determine appropriate course of action, including the ability to extract and analyze information from a variety of sources.

Context: In Rota, Spain, I accepted an administrative office position with an outdated filing system and library of regulations. The files and regulations had not been organized or touched since the 1960s. The filing room was almost totally unusable with stacks of file folders, documents, and regulations approximately 8 feet tall.

Challenge: The files and library of regulations included more than 20 file cabinets and an entire wall of regulations. There were more than 250 notebooks of regulations and documents pertaining to personnel, readiness, payroll, and travel, which were significant when problem solving and researching complex cases of entitlement and pay issues.

Actions: I revamped and updated the unit's outdated filing system and library of regulations, bringing it in accordance with Navy regulations. I also developed an Excel spreadsheet which covered the regulations in the document room. This Excel file took one month to create with categories based on documents in the document library.

Results: This contributed to a 100 percent rating in a later Inspector General's (IG) inspection. Also, the reorganization of the files resulted in extensive time-savings for the CO and XO almost every day. Received recognition and cash award for this service contribution.

3. Ability to communicate orally.

Context: In my current position in Rota, Spain, I am the lead administrative assistant to the CO and XO for the U.S. Naval Base. I am experienced in representing the office with administrative information related to schedules, travel, and problem solving. I enjoy communicating with military personnel, family members, senior officers, and contractors.

An example of a particular experience where I demonstrated empathy and compassion in communications includes:

At Coronado NAS, I had the honor to be a volunteer administrative member of the first Warrior in Transition Program for the base.

Challenge: The major challenges were that this was the first organization of this type for Coronado and required interviewing and assessing the needs of the returning military and family members from Iraq and Afghanistan.

Actions: I was trained to provide advocacy and services to family members to support special needs regarding health care services, critical medical services, and support for medical care. I communicated with military personnel and family members to refer services for medical care and assistance.

Results: The program is now established, and procedures and resources are set up for family members and military personnel who may be needing support from the Warrior in Transition Program. Coronado NAS has approximately 100 service members in the Wounded in Transition Program presently.

KSA SAMPLE 2 - Another Short KSA / Essays / Example

MILITARY SERVICE MEMBER, E-6, US Navy
Target: Supply Specialist, GS-9/11

1. Knowledge of the principles, methods, techniques, and concepts of supply program areas (Commodity Standardization, Inventory Management, Supply Systems Analysis, Supply Administration).

In my roles in the US Navy, I provided oversight leadership and management for logistics, property book / accountability, Supply Administration, Quality Assurance, and inventory management, acquisition, and procurement operations with responsibility for up to $450 million worth of line items (7,300+ line items), including equipment and supplies. I develop logistical program and operational concepts, methods, and techniques required for program execution in the Pacific region. Currently as a Supply Quality Assurance Supervisor, I supervise 71 personnel supporting major logistical programs and inter/intra-service support agreements ensuring the timely support, long-term results, and integration of new and ever evolving Maintenance, Transportation, Supply and Services including IT, Military Clothing and Sales, Warehousing, Food Services, Commercial Industrial-type Functions, Property Accountability, Materiel Readiness, and Supply Management / Operations, HAZMAT, and Fuel Operations for the Pacific region.

Specifically, I planned and coordinated 22 underway (ship) replenishments supporting Operation Iraqi Freedom. I personally determined the distribution and positioning of 7,447 pallets; and I directed the loading, unloading, and delivery of supplies among 41 geographically separated organizations. Following, I conducted customer assistance visits to ensure delivery and determine requirements for distribution. Many of these deliveries ensured life support to personnel in war zones.

2. Ability to communicate in writing.

I write daily. I prepare and write technical and narrative reports, specialized reports, personnel counseling statements, procurement actions, Standard Operating Procedures, policy and procedural documents, operating manuals, and curriculum. I identify training needs and develop performance standards. I plan work schedules, deadlines, and monitor work; coordinate and integrate work schedules; and track progress. I evaluate work performance, provide advice and counsel, manage administrative requirements, and hear and resolve employee complaints.

In a specific example, as the Supply Quality Assurance First Line Supervisor, I designed a supply management inspection checklist for all 167 functional areas of supply and included 570 spot checks, ensuring all areas of supply procedures, policy, and methods were audited monthly. I converted the checklist and produced a handbook ensuring SOPs were managed as a daily practice. The written handbook was adopted as a model for all six Pacific Fleet Aircraft Carriers in the region.

Factor 1: Ability to develop and maintain effective working relationships with all levels of employees, internal/external customers, and a small group of EEO professionals to effectively execute or promote a successful program.

Introduction
In addition to managing equal employment programs for more than 5 years, I have managed projects and programs in the area of civilian personnel which required developing and maintaining effective working relationships with employees, managers, and colleagues.

Context:
As an EEO Officer at Headquarters, U.S. Army Materiel Command (AMC), I was tasked with researching, developing, and establishing a Separate Reporting Activity for the Equal Employment Office at the Headquarters, U.S. Army Materiel Command (AMC).

Challenge:
The major challenge of the new Report and the Activity to create the Report was to gain cooperation for the systematic collection of EEO case numbers from EEO officers and military personnel worldwide. Gaining cooperation would involve communications, advocacy, training, and managing effective working relationships with points of contacts at every Army base.

Actions:
I researched current EEO case reporting methods, past spreadsheets, and analysis of total cases and devised a plan of action to write a new survey. I established the interest of senior offices through <u>ongoing working relationships with senior military and civilian officers</u>. I presented and marketed the new concept plan within the AMC Command Group that consisted of several Brigadier Generals, Major Generals, Lieutenant Generals and one four-star General, the Secretary of the Army for Manpower & Reserve Affairs, Senior Executive Service Officers, and other key officials.

Results:
As a result of our team efforts and the informative and persuasive presentation, the concept plan for the Separate Reporting Activity and the Separate Report was approved by higher headquarters and the Separate Reporting Activity was established at the Headquarters. The Reports are now used to analyze EEO reports, cases, and results worldwide. I received a recognition for Outstanding Service, including "recognized for resourcefulness in <u>achieving Army-wide cooperation</u> for a new process that will result in higher quality workplace for employees," from David Smith, Director, EEO.

KSA SAMPLE 4 - KSAs in the Resume in the Outline Format

With Army, AF, Navy, and other resume-only applications, the instructions will ask you to include "KSAs in the resume." Here are two ways to clearly give examples to support KSAs in the resume. Use ALL CAPS to feature some of the keywords from the KSA in your resume, so that the human resources specialist and the supervisor can clearly see your qualifications for the position.

Sample KSAs in the resume vacancy announcement instructions:

Defense Intelligence Agency

Financial Services Support Technician
Department: Department Of Defense
Agency: Defense Intelligence Agency
SERIES & GRADE: IA-0503-B02/B02

> This is a temporary position

QUALIFICATIONS REQUIRED:

Mandatory Assessment Factors to be covered in the resume
1. Recognizes when others need assistance and responds with positive support to advance team or unit goals.
2. Uses a variety of media and presentation modes to convey different types of information.
3. Understands factors that may lead to incomplete data sets and proactively addresses gaps in information.
4. Demonstrate ability reviewing automated financial documentations/reports to ensure the accuracy of data and compliance with regulations.
5. Prepares responses to standard tasks by applying a full range of specialized processes, databases, and/or systems pertinent to a budget execution.

Federal Resume in the Outline Format with KSAs / Assessment Factors / Keywords in ALL CAPS

JOHN RODRIQUEZ
12500 Wilson Boulevard, #320
San Diego, CA 92126
Phone: (858) 555-0000
Email: JRod2005@aol.com

PROFESSIONAL EXPERIENCE

November 1008 – January 2010, ACCOUNTING CHIEF, E-6, 40+ hrs per week
U.S. Marine Corps, AC/S Comptroller, Bldg 1160, Camp Pendleton, CA 92055-5010
Supervisor: Lt. Col Nathan Kojak (retired); (760) 555-8888; May be contacted.

Promoted from E-1 to E-6 through series of increasingly responsible assignments. Each level included developing and delivering various training modules, establishing fund administrators, planning, budgeting, auditing fund administrator accounts, and communicating comptroller requirements to organizations within the scope of the comptroller.

TEAM LEAD TO ACHIEVE UNIT GOALS: Supervised 5-10 military and civilian personnel having a variety accounting functions. Recognize when others need assistance. Exercised full supervisory authority and discretion for military personnel; advised managers on civilian employees' performance for annual review. Mentored and counseled civilian employees regarding performance and opportunities for promotion.

UTILIZE VARIOUS MEDIA TO PRESENT BRIEFS TO SENIOR MANAGEMENT: Brief the upper management concerning $10-20 million in accounting data, including military personnel records pertaining to performance reports. Reviewed and analyzed accounting functions including presenting and executing operating budget to ensure valid data. Utilize PowerPoint, Graphics, charts and multi-media to present details and objectives

AUTOMATED FINANCIAL DOCUMENTS AND REPORTS. Applied knowledge of rules, regulations, and government policies to write and edit 30-45 fund administrator requests annually. Analyzed budget data and budget requests. Ensured budgets were processed correctly in accounting system. Advised decision-makers on alternative methods of funding, spending, and accounting of authorized funds. Annually audited, monitored, and analyzed each executed budget for authorized spending.

REVIEW AUTOMATED FINANCIAL DOCUMENTS AND REPORTS FOR ACCURACY. Reviewed fund administrators' performance and advised on reprogramming of funds to support new or revised requirements during the course of the fiscal year. Continually reviewed comptroller programs to ensure data, reports, and staffing were at acceptable levels. Delivered training and supplied appropriate reference materials to correct misunderstandings of accounting systems and procedures.

PREPARE RESPONSES TO STANDARD TASKS WITH DATABASES AND SYSTEMS PERTINENT TO BUDGET. Coordinated and supervised fund administrator audit teams that conducted reviews to oversee each authorized budget. Maintained and reconciled official accounting records, including official accounting reports after each accounting cycle.

Prepare responses to standard tasks by applying review of databases pertinent to budget execution. Designed and delivered training, including step-by-step instructions, tested for impromptu application, the application now used as the standard for data retrieval in U.S. Marine Corps accounting system.

KEY ACCOMPLISHMENTS: Served as initial point of contact for establishment of Oracle-based SABRS Management Analysis Retrieval Tool System (SMARTS) application. Trained 30-40 personnel prior to launching application on individual computers. Coordinated technical phone assistance and troubleshooting. Modified training module to suit specific needs of three major military commands.

THE IMPORTANCE OF A GOOD COVER LETTER

> The White House, Office of the Press Secretary
> For Immediate Release, May 11, 2010
> Presidential Memorandum -- Improving the Federal Recruitment and Hiring Process:
>
> *"...allow individuals to apply for Federal employment by submitting resumes and cover letters or completing simple, plain language applications, and assess applicants using valid, reliable tools..."*

Cover letters are now officially part of the federal application!

Specialized Experience
Add a list of skills and experience that you can offer that matches the Specialized Experience in the announcement.

Passion and Interest in the Mission
Write about your interest in the mission of the agency or organization. If you know the mission, can speak about it in a sentence, you can stand out above your competition.

Letter of Interest
The cover letter IS a letter of interest. You are interested in the job. The cover letter is more than a transmittal. Take this opportunity to sell your special qualifications, certification, training and mission-related experiences to stand out. This is another small writing test.

Adding or Uploading a Short Cover Letter Into the Resume Builder
With USAJOBS, you can add the letter in to Additional Information section. With CPOL, you can add the cover letter into Other Information section. With applicationmanger.gov, you can upload your cover letter.

Special Considerations
You can mention your willingness to relocate, eligibility for non-competitive spouse appointments, veteran's preference, reasons for wanting to move, such as family, and other special interest items in the cover letter.

Why Hire Me?
Be sure to mention your best qualities (that match the announcement).

Compelling?
Tell the reader why you are an excellent candidate and you believe in the mission of the agency.

Be sure to include announcement qualifications in your cover letter, such as: providing assistance to senior specialists in the evaluation and analysis of training programs; assisting in the execution of training programs by carrying out specified portions or segments of specific projects (e.g., preparing and coordinating training requests, advertising upcoming training, maintaining training attendance data, arranging training spaces and locations, identifying training needs and informing staff of upcoming training classes); and identifying and recommending solutions to training problems and providing advice to staff on established methods and procedures.

MELODY ANN RICHARDS
2222 Alexandria Boulevard
Falls church, VA 22043
Phone: 703-333-3333
Email: _melody.richards@army.mil_

US Department of State
Application Evaluation Branch
2401 E Street, NW
Washington, DC 20522-0108
ATTN: John Jones
RE: MISSION SUPPORT SPECIALIST (TRAINING), Annct No: 30303

Dear Mr. Jones:

Enclosed are my application materials for the Mission Support Specialist (Training Coordinator) within the Foreign Service Institute, Department of State.

I can offer the Foreign Service Institute the following training and program coordination skills:

- Evaluating and analyzing training programs and curriculum
- Coordinating training programs by professional instructors
- Managing training space, training equipment needs
- Managing registrations and attendance
- Identifying and recommending training solutions to individuals and managers
- Recommending training techniques to improve evaluations and customer satisfaction

One of my strongest assets as a training administrator is my ability to manage complex international courses and programs and resolve problems related to instructors, curriculum, and technology.

I am dedicated to helping to coordinate international training programs for Department of State and other foreign affairs agencies to assist employees transitioning from full-time government work due to retirement or involuntary separation. I am highly detailed and can offer diplomacy and tact in communicating with State Department professionals and Foreign Service Officers.

I am willing to travel if needed and am planning to relocate to the DC area next month. I am available for an interview at your convenience.

Sincerely,
MELODY ANN RICHARDS

Currently, there are many ways to apply for federal jobs. If you have both a paper federal resume and an electronic resume prepared, you should be ready to apply to all of the jobs in their various required formats. After you apply to a few of the announcements, you will get faster and be able to adjust your resume to fit the application requirements.

Read the "how to apply" instructions, they could be different for each announcement. Get ready to copy and paste into builders, answer questions, write short essays, and fax or upload DD-214 and transcripts. Apply a day early if possible to navigate the automated application systems.

Be patient and consider each job and agency separately. Your perseverance will pay off. Learn how to copy and paste quickly. Use the control-A (copy all), control-C (copy), and control-V (paste) characters. This will speed up your copy and paste submissions.

On left: screenshot of Kathryn Troutman's USAJOBS profile page.

For most of the automated applications, you have to set up an account and answer important personnel profile questions about your federal job preferences. For instance, you will need an account in both USAJOBS and Application Manager.

Federal Resume in USAJOBS + Assessment Questionnaire

This format is the most popular application method today. First you will begin by submitting your resume in USAJOBS, then you will click on APPLY NOW, and USAJOBS will automatically direct you to an automated assessment questionnaire systems such as Application Manager or Quickhire.

Federal Resume in USAJOBS + KSAs that are rated & ranked

When applying in USAJOBS, sometimes you will still see instructions for writing KSAs on "separate sheets of paper". These KSAs will be submitted in various ways: online, by email, or through a short online questionnaire form. These "rated and ranked" KSAs could be eliminated this year.

Federal Resume and Assessment

Avuecentral is a separate automated recruitment system used by about 30 federal agencies. You will find the job announcement on USAJOBS, but then you will go automatically to Avuecentral to set up an account, submit your resume, complete the assessment questionnaire, and fax documents to the Avue system.

Resumix + Supplemental Database

Army (CPOL), Navy (DONHR), and DOD (WHS) are using Resumix for their automated recruitment system. This is a keyword system; the first "cut" of qualified candidates will be searched for with 5 to 7 keywords found in the announcement. You will submit a resume, supplemental statement, and self-nomination. No questionnaires or KSAs are required.

Paper Federal Resumes

Occasionally, you are asked to email or send your resume. This resume format can be the USAJOBS version (by previewing and saving the USAJOBS builder resume) or a paper format resume formatted similar to a private industry resume. Make sure to include the compliance details required by the human resources office.

Optional Form OF-612

The OF-612 was designed in 1995 to replace the SF-171. All of the information that you will write in your federal resume will also be listed in the OF-612. The problem is that the form is rigid for the applicant and difficult to use. If you have a choice to use a resume rather than the OF-612, use the federal-style resume as shown in this book. The fillable OF-612 is available on the OPM website.

★ AGENCY RESUME BUILDER CHART

Name of Agency	Agency Jobs Website	Resume Builder	Questionnaire System	Job Blocks/ Character Limit	Features
USAJOBS/ OPM	www.usajobs.gov	USAJOBS	Application Manager	No limit/3,000	Add'l Info, 22,000 char
Agriculture	www.usda.gov/da/employ/director.htm	USAJOBS	Application Manager	No limit/3,000	Add'l Info, 22,000 char
Air Force	www.usajobs.gov	USAJOBS	Application Manager	No limit/3,000	
Army	www.cpol.army.mil	CPOL	N/A	12,000 total	One field for work exp.
AVUE CENTRAL	www.avuecentral.com	AVUE	AVUE	No limit/4,000	PDs available
Bureau of Land Management	www.blm.gov/jobs	USAJOBS	Quickhire	No limit	
Central Intelligence Agency	https://www.cia.gov/careers/index.html	CIA Builder	CIA	1,000	Short
Commerce	www.commerce.gov/JobsCareerOpportunities/index.htm	USAJOBS	mgsapps. monster.com	No limit/3,000	
Defense Contract Management Agency	www.dcma.mil/careers.htm	CPOL	CPOL Builder	12,000 total	Paste your work
Defense Finance & Accounting Office	www.dfas.mil/careers/post/resumebuilderinfo.html	DFAS Resume Builder	DFAS	No limit/No limit	
Defense Logistics Agency	www.hr.dla.mil/prospective	USAJOBS	Application Manager	No limit/No limit	
Education	www.ed.gov/about/jobs/open/edhires/index.html	USAJOBS	Quickhire	3,000 characters	Paste a resume, 16K char total
Energy	www.energy.gov/careers@energy.htm	USAJOBS or Paper	Quickhire	No limit/3,000 or Paper (N/A)	Different Hiring Processes - Quickhire
Environmental Protection Agency	www.epa.gov/ezhire	USAJOBS	EZ Hire	No limit/3,000	
FAA	https://jobs.faa.gov/asap	ASAP	ASAP	4,000	15 minute limit
FBI	www.fbijobs.gov	FBIJOBS	Quickhire	No limit/No limit	Paste a resume, 16K char total
Forest Service	www.fs.fed.us/fsjobs/openings.html	AVUE	AVUE	No limit/4,000	PDs available
Government Accountability Office	www.gao.gov/jobopp.htm	USAJOBS	Quickhire	No limit/3,000	Paste a resume, 16K char total
General Services Administration	www.gsa.gov	GSA Jobs	Quickhire	No limit	Paste a resume, 16K char total
Health & Human Services	www.hhs.gov/careers	HHS Careers/ USAJOBS	Quickhire	No limit	Paste a resume, 16K char total
HHS National Institutes of Health	www.training.nih.gov/careers/careercenter	NIH/HHS Careers / USAJOBS	Quickhire	No limit	Paste a resume, 16K char total
Homeland Security	www.dhs.gov/xabout/careers	USAJOBS	Various	No limit/3,000	Add'l Info, 22,000 char
Citizenship & Immigration Services	www.uscis.gov/portal/site/uscis	USAJOBS	Application Manager	No limit/3,000	Add'l Info, 22,000 char

Name of Agency	Agency Jobs Website	Resume Builder	Questionnaire System	Job Blocks/ Character Limit	Features
Customs & Border Protection	www.cbp.gov/xp/cgov/careers	USAJOBS	Application Manager	No limit/3,000	Add'l Info, 22,000 char
FEMA	www.fema.gov/career	USAJOBS	Application Manager	No limit/3,000	
Housing & Urban Development	jobsearch.usajobs.opm.gov/a9hudp.asp	USAJOBS/Paper	Application Manager/ paper	No limit/3,000 Paper - no limit	
Interior	www.doi.gov/doijobs/jobs.html	USAJOBS	USAJOBS	No limit/3,000	
Justice	www.usdoj.gov	AVUE	AVUE	No limit/4,000	PDs available
Labor	www.dol.gov/dol/jobs.htm	USAJOBS	DOORS	No limit/3,000	
National Aeronautics & Space Administration	www.nasajobs.nasa.gov	USAJOBS	STARS	No limit/3,000	6 page resume limit (22,000 characters)
National Security Agency	www.nsa.gov/home_html.cfm	NSA Careers	None		Full text resume
Navy	https://chart.donhr.navy.mil	Navy CHART	None	6/6,000	
Office of Secretary of Defense	https://storm.psd.whs.mil/WHSJobs.html	HRD Resumix	None	no info	Paste a resume
Peace Corps	www.avuecentral.com	AVUE	AVUE	No limit/4,000	PDs available
Small Business Administration	www.usajobs.gov	Paper	Paper	No limit	Flexible
State Department	careers.state.gov	Various Methods	Paper	No limit	Various application methods, including forms
Transportation	careers.dot.gov	USAJOBS/Paper	Quickhire	No limit	Paste a resume, 16K char total
Transportation Security Agency	www.usajobs.gov	Paper	Paper	No limit	Flexible/paper
US Marshals Service	www.avuecentral.com	AVUE	AVUE	No limit/4,000	PDs available
Veterans Affairs	www.va.gov/jobs/Career_Search.asp	USAJOBS/Paper	Paper	No limit/3,000	Online or paper
Washington Headquarters Services	www.whs.mil/HRD	HRD Resumix	N/A	4 pages + Supp	

Disclaimer: Please know that resume builders, agency career website addresses, methods of collecting resumes, and other information may change from week to week.

USAJOBS allows a jobseeker to have up to five versions of the resume in the database at once. This makes focusing your resume on a particular job series very easy. You can update your resumes in USAJOBS as often as you like. It is a rigid format in that, if you wanted to list education before experience, or put your work experience out of chronological order, you would not be able to do that.

Putting a resume in USAJOBS does not mean that you have applied to a job; you are simply storing your resume in the database for later use. You must click "APPLY ONLINE" to start an actual application.

For some announcements, the USAJOBS resume, along with the supplemental data section, is the whole application. For others, the USAJOBS resume is used in tandem with another online system or faxed documents. Follow each step in sequence until you receive a confirmation that your application was sent.

TIP: Put your resume into the USAJOBS online database BEFORE starting an application.

Step by Step: USAJOBS Resume and Application

1. Create a USAJOBS account and fill in your profile information.

2. Use the resume builder in "MY USAJOBS" to create your federal resume. There are many sections to fill in besides work experience and education. Provide as much information as you can that will show your qualifications for the job. You can have up to five different versions in the system at once.

> **Warning about USAJOBS Upload Resume feature:** If you upload a Word resume, the resume may not be forwarded to applicationmanager.gov, or other questionnaire system. It might be better to use the USAJOBS Resume Builder.

3. Find your announcement and determine whether you can apply by checking the "who can apply" section.

4. After your resume is in the system, click "APPLY ONLINE" to start the application process.

5. USAJOBS will ask you which version of your resume you want to use for that particular application. Select the one targeted for that job.

6. If the application requires you to complete information on an additional website, your browser will take you there.

7. Follow all steps through final submission.

USAJOBS Resume Builder – Five Resumes

You can store up to five different resumes on USAJOBS. If you analyze your keywords for more than one job series, you might want to have different resume versions naming the resume with that job title.

This automated system, run by USA Staffing, is frequently used in conjunction with USAJOBS, where https://applicationmanager.gov is the utility for administering the self-assessment and supplemental data questions. You will have the choice of pulling your resume

from the USAJOBS online database, or you can upload your resume file. The upload allows greater flexibility in your resume presentation because you can format it however you like.

Step by Step: Application Manager with USAJOBS Resume Retrieval

1. Create a USAJOBS account and fill in your profile information.

2. Use the resume builder in "MY USAJOBS" to create your federal resume.

3. Find your announcement and click "APPLY ONLINE" to start the application process.

4. USAJOBS will ask you which version of your resume you want to use for that particular application. Select the one targeted for that job.

5. Your browser will then direct you to applicationmanager.org to complete the biographical and eligibility information and start the Assessment Questionnaire. You will see that you must create a separate login for Application Manager.

6. Complete all questions and follow all steps including "UPLOAD DOCUMENTS." You will not upload a resume or KSA documents, however, you may need to upload or fax supplemental documents like transcripts or veterans forms.

7. Follow all steps through "SUBMIT MY ANSWERS," or your application will not be submitted.

Step by Step: Application Manager with Resume Upload

1. Go to https://applicationmanager.org and create your login and Profile.

2. Enter the job announcement number or USAJOBS control number (found in the USAJOBS vacancy announcement) to retrieve your target vacancy application.

3. Start the application and complete the biographical and eligibility information as well as the Assessment Questionnaire.

4. Upload and/or fax your resume and other pertinent application documents as well as other information that they might request—last evaluation, DD-214 (veterans), and transcripts, for example.

5. Follow all steps through "SUBMIT MY ANSWERS," or your application will not be submitted.

avuecentral

This commercial system is used by more than 30 agencies, including the U.S. Forest Service and U.S. Coast Guard. This application is a complex online form with questions and a profile. You submit your resume one time, and then apply for as many positions in the database that Avue Central maintains. However, this can only be done for vacancies in agencies using this system.

Most jobs posted on AvueCentral.com are also posted on USAJOBS. That means that you can search for them in USAJOBS, where there is greater search flexibility and ease of use, and then apply to them through AvueCentral.com as instructed. You can go to AvueCentral.com directly; however, it is often easier to access the application by starting in USAJOBS and clicking "APPLY ONLINE."

Step by Step: AvueCentral

1. From the USAJOBS vacancy, click "APPLY ONLINE" and your browser will direct you to that particular vacancy in AvueCentral.com or you can go directly to the Avue Central home page and search for the vacancy.

2. Log on or create your Profile in AvueCentral.com. Click "APPLY NOW" to start the application process.

3. On the left side of the screen, you will see a menu for filling in Mandatory information, such as your work history, education, and KSAs. The application will automatically pull your resume information from your Profile, however you also have the option to revise it for the particular application.

4. Each vacancy announcement in Avue Central has "Job Posting Information" that includes the description that you saw posted in USAJOBS as well as the actual position description. Use this information to identify your keywords and write your resume content.

5. Once you have completed every section in Mandatory Information, you will click "SEND APPLICATION" to complete the process.

The U.S. Navy's CHART and Army's CPOL systems are both keyword systems called RESUMIX. The human resources specialist will search for the best qualified people based on keywords that are found in either the vacancy announcement or other sources (as described in Step 4, Find the Perfect Job Announcement).

Open Continuously – Inventory Building – Database Building Announcements. The Navy announcements have very short "duty" descriptions and list multiple job titles in an occupational series. These are databases where HR professionals will search for qualified candidates when positions become available. These are valuable and real announcements. If you are qualified for these positions, you should submit your resume to these databases.

The Army announcements have excellent descriptions of duties and specialized experience. You can find a good keyword description in Army announcements.

Self-Nomination Process

If your resume is already in the database, you can simply "self-nominate" for a special position that interests you. The Navy uses both Open Continuously announcements and special announcements with closing dates. You will not need to resend or re-submit your resume to the particular database. Make sure your resume is in the right database.

Step by Step: CHART or CPOL

1. Create a profile in the pertinent system and fill in your biographical and supplemental data information.

2. Write the correct length resume, paying special attention to whether your content fits within the character limitations.

3. Paste your resume into the online system ahead of the deadline. Sometimes there are special instructions about how far in advance your resume needs to be submitted.

4. Self-nominate for the job according to the agency's instructions.

5. The Supplemental Data Sheet is now part of the builder and you will complete it online. This is very important in that it shows your eligibility for certain jobs based on whether you have status.

Agencies that are still using paper applications may allow several options for your application format. The package usually contains the following: cover letter, federal resume, KSAs, and supplemental information (such as transcripts).

The package is typically mailed, faxed, or hand delivered. You may use the U.S. Postal Service, or other delivery method to transport your package.

We recommend that you use the preferred paper format, a federal resume. Also in the announcement, usually at the end, is the address to which to send your materials, a number to which to fax it, and perhaps instructions on how to apply with email. If you mail your application, get a delivery confirmation receipt. If you are facing a deadline, fax or email will deliver your application the same day. Whatever the method, if you send your materials ahead of the deadline, you will have time to phone the office to confirm receipt.

Your paper application should include the following:
- ☐ A nicely formatted federal resume printed on good quality paper
- ☐ KSA narratives (a separate document)
- ☐ A cover letter (if allowed)
- ☐ Include copies of required supplemental information such as photocopies of transcripts

A human resources specialist will receive your envelope, review the resume for basic qualifications and status, and then rate and rank your KSAs manually by reading for keywords and content. The top candidates will be referred to the hiring supervisor.

Step by Step: Non-Automated Applications

1. Focus your federal resume (with formatting) on the announcement, picking up the keywords and top skills from the duties, qualifications, and evaluation sections.

2. Add the job title, grade, series, and announcement number to the top of the resume and KSAs. Also, always include your name and the last four digits of your Social Security Number.

3. Write your KSAs for the position.

4. Mail, fax, or email your application to the address (follow their directions). Never use a government postage-paid envelope.

5. Send other information that they may request such as last performance evaluation (if you have one—not mandatory), transcripts, and DD-214. Do not send any attachments if they do not ask for any.

Resume Builder

USAJOBS' Resume Builder allows you to create a uniform resume that provides all of the information required by government agencies. Instead of creating multiple resumes in different formats, you can build your resume once and be ready for all job opportunities.

I. Getting Started   2. Experience   3. Related Information   4. Finishing Up

PLEASE NOTE: Fields with an asterisk (✳) are **required fields**.   Click on the ❓ after each title for **more information**.

Confidentiality ❓

Select **confidential** to hide your contact information, current employer name, and references from recruiters performing resume searches.

○ Confidential ⊙ Non-Confidential

Candidate Information ❓

Note: If your resume is **confidential**, this information will not be visible to recruiters performing resume searches.

✳ **Name Your Resume**	[_____]	What is this?
✳ **First Name**	[_____]	
Middle Name	[_____]	
✳ **Last Name**	[_____]	
✳ **Social Security Number**	***-**-6434 Edit Social Security Number	
✳ **Home Address**	[_____]	
Home Address 2	[_____]	
✳ **City/Town**	[_____]	
✳ **State/Territory/Province**	Virginia ⬍	
✳ **Home Postal/ZIP Code**	[_____]	
✳ **Country**	US ⬍	
✳ **Email**	[_____]	
✳ **Phone Numbers**	Day Phone ⬍ [_____]	
	Mobile ⬍ [_____]	
	– SELECT – ⬍ [_____]	
✳ **Are you a U.S. Citizen?**	⊙ Yes ○ No	
✳ **Do you claim veterans' preference?**	○ Yes ⊙ No Does this apply to me?	
Selective Service	☐ Check this box if you are an adult male born on or after January 1st 1960, and you registered for Selective Service between the ages of 18 through 25.	

Highest Career Level Achieved ❓

Note: This will change the Career Level on all your resumes.

Experienced (Non-Manager) ⬍

Federal Employee Information ❓

✳ Are you or were you ever a Federal civilian employee?
○ Yes ⊙ No

Work Experience ❓

Note: If your resume is **confidential**, the name of your current employer (indicated by an end date of "present") will not be visible to recruiters performing resume searches.

✳ **Employer Name** `[                    ]`

✳ **City/Town** `[                    ]`

✳ **State/Territory/Province** `[                    ]`

✳ **Country** `[ US                ▲▼ ]`

✳ **Formal Title** `[                    ]`

✳ **Start Date** `[ May   ▲▼ ] [ 2010 ▲▼ ]`

✳ **End Date:** `[ – SELECT – ▲▼ ] [ Present ▲▼ ]`

Salary `[ $00.000        ]` `[ USD ▲▼ ]` `[ Per Year ▲▼ ]`

✳ **Average Hours per week** `[                    ]`

May we contact your supervisor? ○ Yes ⦿ No ○ Contact me first

Is this a Federal position? ○ Yes ⦿ No

✳ **Duties, Accomplishments and Related Skills**

```
[                                        ]
[                                        ]
[                                        ]
[                                        ]
[                                        ]
```

Problems with formatting when pasting from Word?
Character Count: 0   (3,000 character limit)

Spell Check ✓

Save and Add Experience ▶

── **OR** ──────────────────────────────

☐ **I don't have any relevant work experience.**

To edit your work experience, click the employer name below, make your edits, and then click the "Save and Update" button.

READ THIS - important notice before listing your Education!
Only list degrees from schools that have been accredited by accrediting institutions recognized by the U.S. Department of Education or other education that meet the provisions of the Office of Personnel Management's Operating Manual. **Learn more!**

Education ❓

❋ **School or Program Name**

❋ **City/Town**

❋ **State/Territory/Province**

❋ **Country**   [US ▲▼]

❋ **Degree/Level Attained**   [– SELECT – ▲▼]

                                       Degree/Level Clarifications

Completion Date   [▲▼] [▲▼]

Major

Minor

GPA   [   ] of GPA Max. [   ]

Total Credits Earned

System for Awarded Credits   ◯ Semester Hours
                                       ◯ Quarter Hours
                                       ◯ Other [   ]

Honors   [Select ▲▼]

Relevant Coursework, Licensures and Certifications

Problems with formatting when pasting from Word?
Character Count: 0   (2,000 character limit)

(**Spell Check** ✓)

(**Save and Add Education** ▶)

— OR —

☐ **I don't have any relevant education.**

Job Related Training ❓

List the titles and completion date of training courses that are relevant to the position you are seeking.

Problems with formatting when pasting from Word?
Character Count: 0   (max. 5,000 characters)

(**Spell Check** ✓)

References ?

Note: If your resume is **confidential**, this information will not be visible to recruiters performing resume searches.

Name:

Employer:

Title:

Phone:

Email:

Reference Type: ⦿ Professional ○ Personal

Add Reference ▶

Additional Language Skills ?

Language: – SELECT –

Spoken: ⦿ None ○ Novice ○ Intermediate ○ Advanced

Written: ⦿ None ○ Novice ○ Intermediate ○ Advanced

Read: ⦿ None ○ Novice ○ Intermediate ○ Advanced

Add Language ▶

Language	Spoken	Written	Read	
Chinese - Mandarin	Intermediate	Novice	Novice	✄
Japanese	Novice	Novice	Novice	✄

Affiliations ?

Organization Name:

Affiliation/Role:

Add Affiliation ▶

Professional Publications ?

Enter any professional publications in the space provided

Problems with formatting when pasting from Word?
Character Count: 0   (5,000 character limit)

Spell Check ✓

Additional Information ?

Enter job-related honors, awards, leadership activities, skills (such as computer software proficiency or typing speed) or any other information requested by a specific job announcement.

Need more space? Expand this field.

Problems with formatting when pasting from Word?
Character Count: 0   (20,000 character limit)

Spell Check ✓

Availability ❓

Note: Including this information will provide recruiters with additional detail on the type of position you are seeking. It will not exclude your resume from consideration.

What type of work will you be willing to accept?

☐ Permanent   ☐ Temporary   ☐ Term   ☐ Intermittent

☐ Detail   ☐ Temporary Promotion   ☐ Summer   ☐ Seasonal

☐ Federal Career Intern   ☐ Student Career Experience

What type of work schedule will you be willing to accept?

☐ Full Time   ☐ Part Time   ☐ Shift Work

☐ Intermittent   ☐ Job Share

Looking for a Specific Work Environment ❓

Note: Including this information will provide recruiters with additional detail on the type of position you are seeking. It will not exclude your resume from consideration.

Please select your desired work environment

☐ Student   ☐ Undergraduate   ☐ Graduate

☐ Post-graduate   ☐ New Professional   ☐ Mid-Career Professional

☐ Retiree   ☐ Federal Retiree   ☐ Highly Mobile

☐ Revolving   ☐ Term   ☐ Mission-Focused

☐ Experienced Professionals ☐ Requires Flexibilities ☐ Telework

☐ Part-Time   ☐ Alternative Work Schedule

Desired Locations ❓

Note: Including this information will provide recruiters with additional detail on the type of position you are seeking. It will not exclude your resume from consideration. Please select the Desired Location(s) you are willing to work in.
(For multiple locations, hold down the <Ctrl> key (PC) or <Command> key (Mac) as you select.)

Choose State   then Locale(s)   Click arrow to add ('X' to delete)

```
US
Alabama
Alaska
American Samoa
Arizona
Arkansas
Armed Force Europe, the
```

ADD

DELETE

Show locations for this region:
<u>United States</u> | <u>Africa</u> | <u>Asia</u> | <u>Europe</u> | <u>North America</u> | <u>South America</u> | <u>Australia</u> | <u>Caribbean and Central America</u> | <u>Middle East</u>

1. Read specific instructions for each Resume Builder.

2. If your electronic resume is longer than the Resume Builder character requirements, the extraneous characters could be cut off.

3. Be sure to format your electronic resume to be compatible with the builder. You cannot copy and paste a resume with formatting (bold type, bullets, indentations, etc.) into a builder. The resume will possibly be unreadable and could be rejected.

4. Create your resume in a word processing software in order to check for spelling and grammar mistakes. This is also a helpful way to store your documents from which you can cut and paste, as builders time out. All content should be composed in a word processing software, saved there, and then transferred over. Paste or type your information into each block, as you want it to appear on the resume. Many of the builders allow hard returns to leave blank lines between paragraphs.

5. Be aware that characters like bullets and formatting like bold or italics are usually not allowed. In some cases, this formatting can turn to symbols or gibberish. When you need bullets, use a "+" or a "-". Those characters are typically compatible.

6. Count characters in your job blocks and other categories based on the Resume Builder instructions (Word Count from the Tools menu in Microsoft Word is helpful, or cut and paste it into the actual Resume Builder to get the most accurate count). Make sure you count the spaces.

7. Periodically save your resume as you enter it into the builder to avoid losing your information in the event you get timed out.

8. Some online builders and applications have places to indicate your race, national origin, gender, or medical/disability information. This information is NOT required and it will not adversely affect your application if you decline to answer.

Avoiding Application Pitfalls

❏ You can only have one resume in the Army, Navy, and Washington Headquarter Services (WHS) builders at one time. You will have to change keywords carefully submit resumes for announcements with close dates.

❏ If the position is an Army position, you MUST apply with your resume in the CPOL builder. Same for Navy positions and the CHART builder.

❏ If the position is managed and recruited by Avue Central, you must submit and apply directly to Avue Central.

❏ If the position is managed by OPM, and they are using USAJOBS and Application Manager, then you must hit SUBMIT in the system to actually apply for a position.

❏ If you submit your user name and password to USAJOBS incorrectly three times, you will be locked ou You can set up another user name and password on th spot – you do NOT have to write to HELP.

❏ USAJOBS builder allows you to select confidential. Do not select confidential or the supervisor will not be able to see your past employers.

❏ The USAJOBS resumes are searchable by managers, but at the present time, the searchable system is not being used to search for candidates throughout the entire database. Only resumes submitted and position APPLIED FOR will be accessed.

❏ The USAJOBS builder gives you the SAVE option at the bottom of the page ONLY. If you GO BACK with content on that page that is not saved, it will be lost.

❏ The USAJOBS builder gives you 3,000 characters (including spaces) for each job description. If your current job description is longer than 3,000 characters you can continue in the second job block.

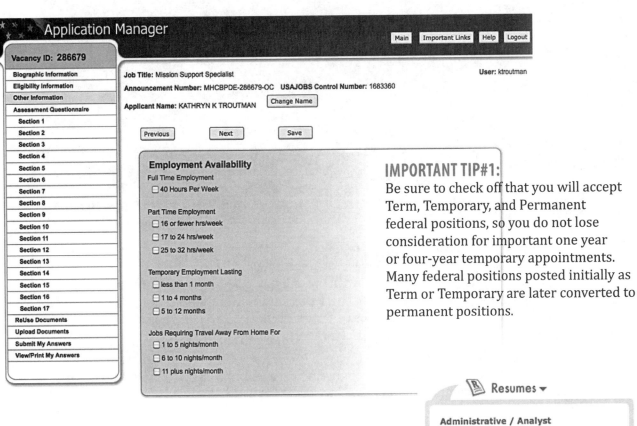

Application Manager

Main | Important Links | Help | Logout

Vacancy ID: 286679

- Biographic Information
- Eligibility Information
- Other Information
- Assessment Questionnaire
  - Section 1
  - Section 2
  - Section 3
  - Section 4
  - Section 5
  - Section 6
  - Section 7
  - Section 8
  - Section 9
  - Section 10
  - Section 11
  - Section 12
  - Section 13
  - Section 14
  - Section 15
  - Section 16
  - Section 17
- ReUse Documents
- Upload Documents
- Submit My Answers
- View/Print My Answers

Job Title: Mission Support Specialist
Announcement Number: MHCBPDE-286679-OC   **USAJOBS Control Number:** 1683360

Applicant Name: KATHRYN K TROUTMAN   [Change Name]

User: ktroutman

[Previous]   [Next]   [Save]

Employment Availability

Full Time Employment
☐ 40 Hours Per Week

Part Time Employment
☐ 16 or fewer hrs/week
☐ 17 to 24 hrs/week
☐ 25 to 32 hrs/week

Temporary Employment Lasting
☐ less than 1 month
☐ 1 to 4 months
☐ 5 to 12 months

Jobs Requiring Travel Away From Home For
☐ 1 to 5 nights/month
☐ 6 to 10 nights/month
☐ 11 plus nights/month

IMPORTANT TIP#1:

Be sure to check off that you will accept Term, Temporary, and Permanent federal positions, so you do not lose consideration for important one year or four-year temporary appointments. Many federal positions posted initially as Term or Temporary are later converted to permanent positions.

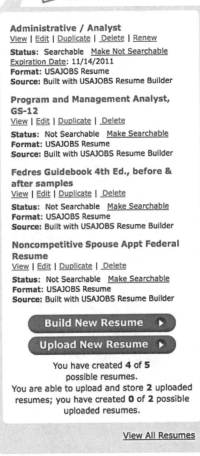

🖹 Resumes ▾

Administrative / Analyst
View | Edit | Duplicate | Delete | Renew
Status: Searchable   Make Not Searchable
Expiration Date: 11/14/2011
Format: USAJOBS Resume
Source: Built with USAJOBS Resume Builder

Program and Management Analyst, GS-12
View | Edit | Duplicate | Delete
Status: Not Searchable   Make Searchable
Format: USAJOBS Resume
Source: Built with USAJOBS Resume Builder

Fedres Guidebook 4th Ed., before & after samples
View | Edit | Duplicate | Delete
Status: Not Searchable   Make Searchable
Format: USAJOBS Resume
Source: Built with USAJOBS Resume Builder

Noncompetitive Spouse Appt Federal Resume
View | Edit | Duplicate | Delete
Status: Not Searchable   Make Searchable
Format: USAJOBS Resume
Source: Built with USAJOBS Resume Builder

[Build New Resume ▶]
[Upload New Resume ▶]

You have created **4** of **5** possible resumes.
You are able to upload and store **2** uploaded resumes; you have created **0** of **2** possible uploaded resumes.

View All Resumes

IMPORTANT TIP #2:

The resume upload feature should only be used for one time and only for one application! Your uploaded resume might NOT get forwarded to the assessment questionnaire system. Also, the uploaded resume might not include all of the compliance details required by that agency. It is recommended to use the resume builder instead!

Learn how to follow up and manage your federal job search campaign. Learn how to call the personnel office and even ask why you weren't Best Qualified. Since the automated systems are so popular with federal agencies now, many of them include an automated reply system, as well as an online page where you can check the status of your applications. This is a great tool. Some people can even read the notice, "you have been offered the position" online.

A federal job applicant can follow up by phone on some job announcements as well. Those that include a name and phone number make follow up possible. It's important to keep track of your applications. Keep the announcements, and follow up on those that include a name and phone number after four to six weeks.

What was your application score?

Here are some scoring benchmarks:
- Highest possible for 10 point veterans: 110
- Highest possible for 5 point veterans: 105
- Highest possible for non-veterans: 100
- Minimally qualified: 70
- Qualified: 80
- Best Qualified: could be 90

What happens to your federal resume and KSA package?

1. Human resources will review your online application and determine if you minimally qualified for the position. With the Resumix (DOD) system, the HR specialist will search with significant keywords and skills for the qualified candidates.
2. If KSAs are required, subject matter experts will examine the KSAs. They will grade the KSAs against a rating schedule or crediting plan. (This will probably be eliminated after November 2010).
3. If Essays are included with the Questionnaires, the HR specialist will read them to determine if you are qualified for the position and if the answers to your questions match your essays.
4. The "best qualified" applicants are referred to the selecting official for consideration and an interview.
7. The selecting official will determine who will be interviewed.

Electronic Applications

Most of the automated application systems have tracking systems where you can check the status of your application. Be sure to check you status regularly. Save your user name and password for each builder.

Find Out Your Application Score – Call, Fax, Email or Write the Personnel Staff

You can contact the human resources specialist to check on the status of your applications and find out what your application score. Whether or not you were referred, knowing your application score will help you determine the next step with your federal job search.

Emails from Human Resources

The May 11, 2010 Presidential Memorandum issued by the White House on *Improving the Federal Recruitment and Hiring Process* says:

> "Notify individuals applying for Federal employment through USAJOBS, an OPM-approved Federal web-based employment search portal, about the status of their application at key stages of the application process … reducing substantially the time it takes to hire mission-critical and commonly filled positions… measuring the quality and speed of the hiring process."

If you receive an email from the HR specialist concerning your qualifications for the position and you can't understand the email, just write back or call to get clarification of the email.

What if You Get a "You Are Qualified" Letter?

If you receive a letter from personnel stating that you did not rate high enough to be referred to the position, that means you didn't make it for this position. But keep trying. If you get a letter saying you are "Qualified" that means you were minimally qualified, not "Best Qualified." You should keep applying for other positions.

Paper Applications

Be sure to use a return-receipt mail system so you can be sure that the application was received by a specific person.

Telephone Message Script

> "Hello, I'm Kathryn Troutman. I'm calling regarding my application submitted for announcement number 10505 for Writer-Editor, GS-12. The closing date was 3/31 and I'm checking on the status of the recruitment. I can be reached at 410-744-4324 from 9 until 5, Monday through Friday, Eastern Standard Time. If you get voicemail, you can leave a message regarding the position. Thank you for your time. I look forward to your information."

Emailing the HR Representative

If there is an email address on the announcement, you could try contacting the personnelist by email. I recommend this letter:

> Subject line: Status of announcement 10101
>
> Dear Ms. Jones,
>
> I submitted my Federal resume, KSAs, and evaluation for the position of Writer-Editor, announcement no. 10101 on Dec. 22 by USPS. I'd like to check the status of my application and the recruitment please.
>
> Is it still open and was I found qualified? Thank you very much for your time.
>
> Sincerely,
>
> Kathryn Troutman, SSN: 000-00-0000
>
> Daytime phone: 410-744-4324 (M-F EST) messages okay

🪑 Application Status

IMPORTANT! If you did not apply to the job announcement with your USAJOBS resume through the apply online button, we cannot track your application. It is not possible to track applications in your USAJOBS account when they have been submitted through an agency's application website or through the mail. You can contact the agency that posted the announcement to verify receipt of your application. Each record will be deleted 18 months after Initial Application Date. You may want to print this page for future reference.

Applications 1 to 20   Page: [1] **[2] [3] [4] [5] [6] [7] [8] [9]**   Page 1 of 9

Initial Application Date ▼	Job Summary	Job Status	Agency Name	Last Application Update	Application Status	USAJOBS Uploaded Document Status
5/17/2010	**Resolutions & Receiverships Spec (WIP-PCAM), CG-1101-13** Job Announcement Number: 2010-TSO-ATL-0332 Pay Plan: CG-1101-13/13 Location: US-FL-Jacksonville	Active	Federal Deposit Insurance Corporation	5/17/2010	Application Status not Available	None more information...
5/17/2010	**Realty Specialist** Job Announcement Number: ADS10-R4-DNF-03407DP (PH) Pay Plan: GS-1170-11/09 Location: US-UT-Panguitch	Closed	Forest Service	5/17/2010	Application Status not Available	None more information...
5/17/2010	**MANAGEMENT AND PROGRAM ANALYST** Job Announcement Number: CIS-PJN-344956-ICS Pay Plan: GS-0343-13/12 Location: US-DC-WASHINGTON	Closed	Citizenship and Immigration Services	5/17/2010	Application Incomplete more information...	None more information...
5/14/2010	**Veterans Service Representative** Job Announcement Number: VB347790--MB Pay Plan: GS-0996/07 Location: US-CO-Lakewood	Closed	Veterans Benefits Administration	5/14/2010	Application Status not Available	None more information...
5/14/2010	**Health Insurance Specialist** Job Announcement Number: HHS-CM-CSQ-2010-0045 Pay Plan: GS-0107-13/13 Location: US-MD-Baltimore (Woodlawn)	Closed	Centers for Medicare & Medicaid Services	5/14/2010	Application Status not Available	None more information...
5/14/2010	**Administrative Tech (OA)** Job Announcement Number: NCAN10929543D Pay Plan: YB-0303-01/01 Location: US-DC-DC - Washington	Closed	Army Medical Command	5/14/2010	Application Status not Available	None more information...
5/14/2010	**Administrative Tech (OA)** Job Announcement Number: NCAN10929543D Pay Plan: YB-0303-01/01 Location: US-DC-DC - Washington	Closed	Army Medical Command	5/14/2010	Application Status not Available	None more information...

Application Manager

Main | Important Links | Help | Logout

user: ktroutman

My Application Packages
(Click a row to see a checklist of all the items you need to complete your application package, and the status of each.)

Vacancy ID : 145961   Job Title : SPECIAL ASSISTANT

Status		Modified Date	Closing Date	USAJOBS Control Number
Complete		7/19/2007 8:31:03 AM	07/19/2007	949266

Vacancy ID : 256569   Job Title : Human Resources Specialist

Status		Modified Date	Closing Date	USAJOBS Control Number
Closed - Not Submitted		4/30/2010 12:21:42 PM	04/30/2010	1547584

Vacancy ID : 286679   Job Title : Mission Support Specialist

Status		Modified Date	Closing Date	USAJOBS Control Number
NOT SUBMITTED		5/3/2010 10:52:13 PM	09/21/2010	1683360

Vacancy ID : 308266   Job Title : Physical Scientist DR-1301-2/3/4

Status		Modified Date	Closing Date	USAJOBS Control Number
Closed - Not Submitted		3/31/2010 5:31:51 PM	03/31/2010	1765405

Vacancy ID : 314268   Job Title : INFORMATION TECHNOLOGY SPECIALIST (INFO SEC)

Status		Modified Date	Closing Date	USAJOBS Control Number
NOT SUBMITTED		3/22/2010 8:38:11 PM	06/19/2010	1788232

Vacancy ID : 314477   Job Title : Program Analyst (Section 508), GS-0343-12/13

Status		Modified Date	Closing Date	USAJOBS Control Number
Closed - Not Submitted		4/7/2010 11:04:00 AM	04/07/2010	1825031

Vacancy ID : 318355   Job Title : Management & Program Analyst

Status		Modified Date	Closing Date	USAJOBS Control Number
NOT SUBMITTED		2/22/2010 3:07:49 PM	08/11/2010	1803306

Vacancy ID : 328400   Job Title : Security Specialist, GS-0080-11/12

Status		Modified Date	Closing Date	USAJOBS Control Number
Closed - Not Submitted		4/14/2010 3:37:00 PM	04/16/2010	1840057

Vacancy ID : 332071   Job Title : Paralegal Specialist

Status		Modified Date	Closing Date	USAJOBS Control Number
Closed - Not Submitted		4/17/2010 4:42:11 PM	04/26/2010	1851491

Vacancy ID : 332930   Job Title : PROCUREMENT ANALYST

Status		Modified Date	Closing Date	USAJOBS Control Number
Closed - Not Submitted		4/26/2010 10:39:13 PM	04/26/2010	1871607

Vacancy ID : 333252   Job Title : Staff Assistant

Status		Modified Date	Closing Date	USAJOBS Control Number
Closed - Not Submitted		3/29/2010 3:19:00 PM	03/29/2010	1856004

Vacancy ID : 333427   Job Title : PROGRAM ANALYST (STRATEGIC PLANNER)

Status		Modified Date	Closing Date	USAJOBS Control Number
Closed - Not Submitted		4/30/2010 8:53:49 AM	05/06/2010	1865989

Vacancy ID : 333539   Job Title : Administrative Officer

Status		Modified Date	Closing Date	USAJOBS Control Number
Closed - Not Submitted		5/6/2010 9:27:40 PM	05/07/2010	1883743

ANSWER
Applicant Notification System Web-Enabled Response

STATUS TRACKING

 Tracking History: Below is the latest status of the jobs for which you requested consideration.

NOTE: You will not see the status of your self nomination until after the announcement closes and qualification determinations are made.
See more records >>

7 Records

Announcement #	Position	Location	Organization	Status
NEFS06248432	EXECUTIVE OFFICER,GS - 0301 - 14	FORT HAMILTON / KINGS / NEW YO	NAD, Ofc of the Comm	2006-05-12 - Your resume has been referred to the selecting official for consideration for this vacancy.
NEBA06211834D	OPERATIONS AND PLANS OFFICER,NH - 0301 - 14	PICATINNY / MORRIS / NEW JERSE	PM Soldier Weapons	2006-06-13 - Your resume has been referred to the selecting official for consideration for this vacancy.
NCBV06302531	SUPERVISORY LOGISTICS MANAGEMENT SPECIALIST,NH - 0346 - 4	WARREN / MACOMB / MICHIGAN	Integ Log SPT Ctr, OPNS/SEC	2006-07-27 - You were referred but not selected for this position.
NEAL06198298	INFORMATION SYSTEMS MANAGEMENT SPECIALIST,DE - 0301 - 4	FT MONMOUTH / MONMOUTH / NEW J	SEC, SOFTWARE ENGINEERING CENT	2006-07-06 - Your resume has been referred to the selecting official for consideration for this vacancy.
SCDN06270620	SUPERVISORY LOGISTICS MANAGEMENT SPECIALIST,GS - 0346 - 14	FORT BRAGG / CUMBERLAND / NORT	HQ, JSOC	2006-07-11 - You were referred but not selected for this position.
NCFR06248720	LIAISON OFFICER,GS - 0301 - 14	COLORADO SPGS / EL PASO / COLO	U.S. ARNORTH	2006-05-31 - You were not referred for this position because you were not in the group of best qualified candidates.
NCAS06335180	SUPERVISORY LOGISTICS SUPPORT SPECIALIST,NH - 0301 - 4	FORT BELVOIR / FAIRFAX / VIRGI	PM TECH INFO SERVICE	2006-06-07 - Your resume has been referred to the selecting official for consideration for this vacancy.

Your first goal for the interview is to stand out above the competition with your relevant skills, experiences, and your ability to communicate them to the hiring manager. Second, you want to impress the hiring team that YOU CAN DO THE JOB being offered. And third, you need to demonstrate confidence, interest, and enthusiasm. This combination of solid relevant content and examples, efficient communications skills, and confident delivery method does not come naturally to most people.

It takes practice, research, and preparation for a successful job interview.

You will see typical questions that could be asked in an interview. Most panel members or individual supervisor/interviewers will prepare seven to ten questions. The same questions are asked of all the interviewees. The answers are graded. So, be prepared to give examples that demonstrate your knowledge, skills, and abilities.

If you have written your KSAs from Step 7, the KSA narrative/examples could be the basis of your accomplishments for the Behavior-Based Interview. But you will have to practice speaking about your accomplishments. Even the most seasoned speakers, briefers, and media experts take training in speaking, presentation, and content development. Jobseekers should spend more time writing examples (their "message") that support their best strengths, and practice speaking these elements. A great interview can get you hired. But interviewing is not easy for anyone.

Be prepared for a new interview format, the behavior-based interview. Be prepared to give examples in answers to seven to ten questions that will be situation or experience based. If you have an example of how you lead a team, provided training, or managed a project, be prepared to talk about the project and teamwork. The best answers will be examples that demonstrate your past performance.

Know the paperwork

Know the vacancy announcement, agency mission, and office function. Read your resume and KSAs out loud with enthusiasm. Become convinced that you are very well qualified for the job and that the agency NEEDS you to help achieve their mission.

Do the necessary research

Go online to research the agency, department, and position. Read press releases about the organization. Go to www.washingtonpost.com and search for the organization to see if there are any recent news events.

Practice

In front of a mirror, tape recorder, video camera, family member, friend, anyone who volunteers to listen to you.

Confidence, Knowledge, and Skills

In order to "sell" yourself for a new position, you have to believe in your abilities. Read books and listen to tapes that will help boost your confidence and give you the support you need to "brag" on your work skills. Don't forget or be afraid to use "I"!

Telephone Interview

Prepare as though you are meeting the person in an office. Get dressed nicely, have your papers neatly organized, create a quiet environment, and project a focused listening and communications style. If you are great on the phone, you can get a second interview.

Individual

One-on-one Interview. Prepare for an unknown Q&A format. Prepare your questions and answers ahead of time and be ready. Be friendly, professional, and answer the questions. Practice for this interview.

Group/Panel Interview

Two to six professional staff will interview and observe your answers. This is a difficult interview format, but it is not used too often. Just look at the person asking the question while he or she is speaking. Answer the question by looking at the person asking, but look around the room as well.

Tell Me about Yourself

Write a three-minute introduction that you could use in an interview. It should include information relevant to the position.

A Significant Accomplishment

Write one significant accomplishment that you will describe in an interview:

Select Your Best Competencies

Make a list of your best core competencies:

Write Your Most Critical Skills:

Make a list of your best skills that will be most marketable to this employer:

Typical interview questions will be:

J	Job Related
O	Open Ended
B	Behavior-Based
S	Skill and Competency Based

Competency-Based Sample Interview Questions

Often, an interviewer will ask questions that directly relate to a competency required for the position. Here are some examples.

- **Attention to Detail:** Describe a project you were working on that required attention to detail.

- **Communication:** Describe a time when you had to communicate under difficult circumstances.

- **Conflict Management:** Describe a situation where you found yourself working with someone who didn't like you. How did you handle it?

- **Continuous Learning:** Describe a time when you recognized a problem as an opportunity.

- **Customer Service:** Describe a situation in which you demonstrated an effective customer service skill.

- **Decisiveness:** Tell me about a time when you had to stand up for a decision you made even though it made you unpopular.

- **Leadership:** Describe a time when you exhibited participatory management.

- **Planning, Organizing, Goal Setting:** Describe a time when you had to complete multiple tasks. What method did you use to manage your time?

- **Presentation:** Tell me about a time when you developed a lesson, training, or briefing and presented it to a group.

- **Problem Solving:** Describe a time when you analyzed data to determine multiple solutions to a problem. What steps did you take?

- **Resource Management:** Describe a situation when you capitalized on an employee's skill.

- **Team Work:** Describe a time when you had to deal with a team member that was not pulling his/her weight.

Present your best competencies with a great story or example that demonstrates your real behavior.

LEADERSHIP – Inspires, motivates, and guides others toward strategic/operation goals and corporate values. Coaches, mentors, and challenges staff and adapts leadership style to various situations. Consistently demonstrates decisiveness in day-to-day actions. Takes unpopular positions when necessary. Faces adversity head on. Rallies support and strives for consensus to accomplish tasks. Leads by personal example. Demonstrates concern for employees' welfare and safety, by continuously monitoring and eliminating potentially hazardous or unhealthy work situations.

Can you give me an example where you lead a team?

CONTEXT:

CHALLENGE:

ACTION:

1.

2.

3.

RESULTS:

C

CCAR (Context, Challenge, Action, Results) Format
   accomplishment freewriting, 89
   interview preparation exercise, 125
   KSAs, 88, 90–91, 93
Central Intelligence Agency (CIA), 100
Certification, 37
Change, leading, 56
CHART (Civilian Human Resources Hiring and Recruitment Tool), 99, 105, 112
CIA. See Central Intelligence Agency
Citizenship & Immigration Services, 100
Civilian Human Resources Hiring and Recruitment Tool (CHART), 99, 105, 112
Civilian Personnel Online (CPOL), 80, 99, 105, 112
Clerical jobs
   General Administrative, Clerical, and Office Services jobs group, 23
   PATCO federal jobs, 34
   pay bands, 33
Coalitions, building, 56
Communication
   competency-based sample interview questions, 124
   emailing HR representatives, 116
   telephone message script, 116
Competencies. See also Core competencies
   interview preparation exercise, 125
   sample interview questions based on, 124
Competitive Service jobs, 35
Computer skills, 36
Conflict management
   competency-based sample interview questions, 124
   executive core qualifications, 56
Contact list, 38
Context, Challenge, Action, Results (CCAR) Format
   accomplishment freewriting in, 89
   interview preparation exercise, 125
   KSAs, 88, 90–91, 93
Copyright, Patent, and Trademark jobs group, 26–27
Core competencies, 7, 52, 123
   analyzing for language, 52
   examples, 52
   executive core qualifications, 56
   Senior Executive Service (SES), 56
   U.S. Marine Corps, 57
   Veterans Administration descriptions, 53–55
Cover letters, 96, 97
CPOL (Civilian Personnel Online), 80, 99, 105, 112
Creativity, 54, 56
Crediting Plan, 83
Criminal Investigator: example vacancy announcement, 58
Customer service
   competency-based sample interview questions, 124
   executive core qualifications, 56
   Veterans Administration core competency descriptions, 53
Customs & Border Protection, 101
Customs Inspector positions, 34

D

Database-building announcements, 45, 105
Decisiveness
   competency-based sample interview questions, 124
   executive core qualifications, 56
Defense Contract Management Agency, 100
Defense Department (DOD)
   application system, 99
   sample Outline Format resume with KSAs for, 95
   sample vacancy announcement with KSAs for, 94
Defense Finance & Accounting Office, 100

F

W

Y

ABOUT THE DESIGNER

Paulina Chen

Photo by Emily Troutman

Paulina Chen is actually a "reverse-client" for Kathryn. Paulina went from working for the federal government to a working for a dynamic, small, woman-owned business -- The Resume Place!

During her 10 years at the U.S. Environmental Protection Agency as an Environmental Engineer, Paulina discovered an interest in writing and designing printed materials. She met Kathryn when Kathryn came the EPA as a federal resume consultant. When Paulina expressed a desire to eventually become a freelance graphic designer, Kathryn noticed Paulina's ability to communicate complex information in a straightforward, easy-to-understand way and signed her on to design the interior pages for the first edition of *Ten Steps to a Federal Job*. Now many years later, this team is still collaborating, and the *Jobseeker's Guide 4th Edition* is their ninth book project together. Paulina also designs and manages the website www.resume-place.com.

Paulina's has a degree in Product Design from Stanford University, which gave her the solid technical and aesthetic fundamentals that she applies to her print and web design. She was also certified by the USDA Graduate School in desktop publishing.

Paulina has helped The Resume Place and other clients with writing and designing books, catalogs, logos, business cards, promotional materials, and websites. She can be reached at paulinachen@livingwaterdesigns.com.

ABOUT THE AUTHOR

Kathryn K. Troutman,
Author and President
The Resume Place, Inc.

Founder
Certified Federal Job Search Program

Photo by Emily Troutman

Kathryn Troutman is a leading expert in federal jobs, a hot topic with the change of administration and the current downturn in the economy. She brings over 30 years of experience in this unique marketplace and has the ability to take the complex subject of federal job searching and break it down into understandable steps.

She is the author of the recently-released Second Edition of *Ten Steps to a Federal Job: How to Get a Job in the Obama Administration*, which is updated from the original 2001 issue. The first Ten Steps book was honored as the Best Career Guide of 2002 by the Publishers Marketing Association.

Troutman wrote the first book on the federal resume format in 1995 in response to the government's move to replace the cumbersome SF-171 form with the resume. These days, she is known as the "Federal Resume Guru," and her book, *The Federal Resume Guidebook*, is a best-seller and in its fourth printing. Over 100 US government agencies hire Troutman to speak as a master trainer each year, and her presentations on writing federal resumes are popular.

Troutman has been interviewed by both national print and electronic media outlets on how to get a job in the federal government (and Obama administration). Troutman is also a columnist for eight online federal and military employment websites.

In addition, Troutman is a trainer's trainer. She has established two certification programs for career counselors on federal job searching. A licensed curriculum, based on her Ten Steps, is taught around the world.

Troutman's message is that there are many desirable federal jobs, but you must know the right way to apply. Featured in the second edition of Ten Steps to a Federal Job are 24 jobseekers who took her recommended steps and landed their dream jobs with Uncle Sam.

Besides federal employment, Troutman also with speaks passionately on "Staying Successful with a Small Business" and "Women Entrepreneurs." Troutman's firm, The Resume Place, has been in business for over 25 years, and she and the company continue to grow and evolve.

www.resume-place.com
The Resume Place, Inc.
Your One-Stop Federal Career and Military to Federal Career Resources Center

Online Builders - Tools To Help You Write Federal Applications

- KSA CCAR Builder (including sample) - popular since 1996!
- Federal Resume Builder - designed in 1996
- Cover Letter Builder - designed in 1996

Newsletter Sign-Up - 3 Newsletters - Written and Published Since 1999 by K. Troutman

- Federal Careers for Jobseekers - newsletters with important federal career tips for federal job interviews, negotiating salaries, understanding pay bands and how to negotiate a salary within a pay band, networking and job fair strategies, and more.
- Career Pro Newsletters for Transition and Career Counselors - strategies and tips for training, advising jobseekers, and success stories from training and federal job placement.

Certified Federal Job Search Trainer Program

Ten Steps to a Federal Job Training. Employment readiness counselors and transition counselors can gain certification to teach Ten Steps to a Federal Job to transitioning military and spouses of active duty military. Courses taught on bases and in Columbia, MD near DC annually.

Searchable Federal Career Articles

Kathryn Troutman and the RP team write numerous articles, newsletters, and blogs with the most up-to-date articles and tips for writing federal resumes and applications. Find all of these articles archived here.

FREE Webinars!

Free, one hour webinars with Kathryn Troutman with USAJOBS tours and question and answer sessions.

One-on-One Help? Consider Professional Federal Resume and KSA Services

Writing, Editing, Critique, One-on-One Consulting (via telephone and email) – get expert help! Fee-based services, affordable, flexible, online. You can trust us; we wrote all of these books!